Taking Control of
Your Own
Career

How To Books are designed to help people achieve their goals. They are for everyone wishing to acquire new skills, develop self-reliance, or change their lives for the better. They are accessible, easy to read and easy to act on. Other titles in the series include:

Achieving Personal Well-being
How to discover and balance your physical and emotional needs

Unlocking Your Potential
How to master your mind, life and destiny

Self-Counselling
How to develop the skills to positively manage your life

Building Self-esteem
How to replace self-doubt with confidence and well-being

Controlling Anxiety
How to master fears and phobias and start living with confidence

Career Networking
How to develop the right contacts to help you throughout your working life

The *How To Series* now contains
around 250 titles in the following categories:

Business & Management

Computer Basics

General Reference

Jobs & Careers

Living & Working Abroad

Personal Finance

Self-Development

Small Business

Student Handbooks

Successful Writing

For full details, please send to our distributors for a free copy of the latest catalogue:

How To Books
Customer Services Dept.
Plymbridge House, Estover Road
Plymouth PL6 7PZ, United Kingdom
Tel: 01752 202301   Fax: 01752 202331
http://www.howtobooks.co.uk

Taking Control of
Your Own Career

*Using NLP and other techniques to
get the working life you want*

BARBARA BUFFTON

How To Books

Published by How To Books Ltd., 3 Newtec Place,
Magdalen Road, Oxford OX4 1RE, United Kingdom
Tel: (01865) 793806   Fax: (01865) 248780
email: info@howtobooks.co.uk
www.howtobooks.co.uk

British Library Cataloguing-in-Publication Data
A catalogue record for this book is available from
the British Library

Editing by Alison Wilson
Cover design by Shireen Nathoo Design
Cover image PhotoDisc

Produced for How To Books by Deer Park Productions
Typeset by Euroset, Alresford, Hampshire SO24 9PQ
Printed and bound by Cromwell Press, Trowbridge, Wiltshire

NOTE: The material contained in this book is set out in good
faith for general guidance and no liability can be accepted
for loss or expense incurred as a result of relying in particular
circumstances on statements made in the book. The laws
and regulations are complex and liable to change, and readers
should check the current position with the relevant authorities
before making personal arrangements.

Contents

List of Activities

Preface

Many of us may be in jobs which are no longer a perfect fit with our character, if they ever were. The career intentions we had as young people may no longer suit us as mature adults. Yet we may feel either trapped on a career path or uncertain of which direction to take next. There are also many people wanting to return to work, to do something worthwhile with their lives and others trying to find that all important first job. This book gives useful advice on how to decide what you really want and how to achieve it.

To be employed these days does not necessarily or automatically mean having a permanent, full-time and secure job. Most employers now use part-time, contract and temporary workers, with many employing only a core of permanent full-time staff. Various pieces of labour market research suggest that it is likely that people will change jobs or careers more than once and experience at least one period of unemployment throughout a lifetime. Whether or not this proves to be the case, if individuals take responsibility for their own career development, they will be better prepared for any situation that arises.

This book explains clearly how you can release the potential within you to take that personal responsibility. You will be able to create the working life you want, at whatever age or stage you are at, whether you are employed, looking for work (or a purpose in life) or self-employed.

There are several practical exercises and activities to help you decide what you want and how to access all the resources within and around you. Many techniques are taken from the field of neuro linguistic programming (NLP), a discipline that I believe aims to give you more choices in your life. Read with a healthy scepticism, taking what you find useful and disregarding the rest.

After working for some time, many people are scared to change direction or feel that financial commitments make it impossible to do so. This book looks at how to overcome such obstacles and follow dreams.

Sound advice is given on how to acquire the skills and experience needed for working in the third millennium. Other techniques and exercises throughout the book tap the power of the imagination and the unconscious mind through creative visualisation and affirmations.

This book is for you if you want to achieve positive career and personal goals through using NLP and other personal growth techniques and principles. You do not need any prior knowledge of these methods to gain from this book. You only need yourself, some writing tools and the will to take control of your own career – STARTING NOW!

Acknowledgements

I would like to give credit and recognition to John Grinder and Richard Bandler, co-developers of NLP, and to John Seymour, NLP trainer and author, for much of the inspiration for this book and for many of the techniques shown, although the interpretations are mine alone. My grateful thanks also to the following: my best critic, my husband Barry Mortimer, who has unstintingly offered his love and support and read every word I have written with a constructively critical eye; Gary Deane, my good friend and fellow NLPer for his sound advice and excellent suggestions; Sally Beer, a special person who always gives me encouragement; Sara Mills who helped me start the process; the people whose real life situations inspired the case stories (particularly Val Hood whose story appears in Chapter 8) and finally to my publishers for having faith in me.

Barbara Buffton

1

Knowing Where You Are Now

FACING THE FACTS

'I'm bored...', 'I feel like a change, I'm in a rut', 'I just feel I could do something better than this', 'I'm beginning to dread Monday mornings', 'I want to *do* something with my life'...

Does any of this sound familiar? Thoughts such as these can signal that it is time to move on, to do something different. They may be your first conscious insight into the fact that you are dissatisfied with what you are currently doing. Moving away from painful situations can sometimes be a more powerful motivator than moving towards pleasurable ones. Take note of your thoughts and decide that **today** is the day you will begin to take control of your own career. If you do not, you may be missing out on a compelling and exciting future.

Gaining access to some useful tools

Throughout this book, you will find some principles and examples of techniques taken from Neuro Linguistic Programming (NLP). NLP means different things to different people, because we are all unique individuals. It is sometimes called a form of applied psychology – a way of thinking and behaving. It can also be a way of giving yourself more choices in life through your thoughts, communications and behaviours. One of the major principles of NLP is 'if what you are doing is not working, do something different'. This book may help you define what it is you have to do differently to effect change.

Understanding the basics of NLP

However, this book is not about NLP and does not seek to explain it in great detail. There are many other books and courses which do that quite successfully. Nevertheless, it may be useful to give a definition of the term Neuro Linguistic Programming.

The **Neuro** part of NLP describes how our perception and experience of the world through our five senses (touch/feeling, sight, sound, taste, smell) affect our behaviour. We do not all make sense of the world in the same way. It would be very boring if we did. Have you ever wondered why someone else understood something completely differently to you, when you were both listening to the same thing? Or why you can see clearly something that someone else cannot, even though it is apparently right in front of you both?

One of the reasons is that some of us prefer to take in information more through our eyes, others through our ears and still others through our feelings. We often demonstrate this by our language: we *see* what someone means, or we *hear* what they are saying, or we *get* the message/*grasp* the facts. A few people experience the world primarily through taste or smell, for example, saying that something *fishy* is going on, or it was a *bitter pill* to take.

The fact that our neurology affects our behaviour and our language means that our mind and body are linked. Our mind has been likened to the world's most powerful computer. It is therefore important to know how to use it to our advantage. This will be covered in later chapters.

The **Linguistic** part of NLP is about our use of language and how powerful our words are. Our language can also have a startling effect on our behaviour. This is explored more in Chapter 5.

The **Programming** part explores how we can order or programme our thoughts and behaviours to get the results we want. It is about changing the way we experience and respond to the world.

There are also creative visualisations, affirmations and other practical exercises to help you work out exactly what you want in your life. They will also enable you to work towards your goals, whatever they may be.

Getting ready
You will need your own tools:

- paper (plain allows for more creativity; lined can be restricting)
- pens (coloured if possible)
- a ringbinder or notebook to store your thoughts and dreams
- time and space set aside just for you.

Making any change in your life is a serious business and needs to be given the importance it deserves. It is not something you can do with one eye on the television or one ear listening out for the children or the telephone. It deserves your whole attention. It is your life we are talking about after all. Talk to your family or whoever else is affected by you taking some time out for yourself. Share your ideas with them and ask for their support. Explain the benefits to them of giving you this time and space now. For example, it could make you happier and therefore could make them happier.

However, being serious about something does not mean you cannot have fun at the same time. Imagine you are going on a journey of self-exploration and discovery. Prepare as you would for a journey, by thinking about all the things that would make it more enjoyable and comfortable. For example, put some music on, surround yourself with things that inspire you or that you just like looking at, have some refreshments to hand and get comfortable. Engage all your senses. Be curious and focused, and also enjoy the process you are about to begin.

FINDING OUT WHO YOU REALLY ARE

'Knowing others is intelligence; knowing your self is wisdom.' Lao-Tzu.

Why now?

As you are reading this now, it may be that you have taken that all-important first step and are seriously thinking about making some changes in your life, whatever your age or your situation. People want change for all kinds of reasons. For instance, you may be:

- considering a career change

- searching for a job

- looking for greater job satisfaction

- hoping to return to work

- looking for something worthwhile to do with your time.

Whatever your situation, you have decided that now is the time to take control of your career. It is an appropriate time to do this, given that the nature of work has shifted over the years and individuals are now largely having to be responsible for their own career development.

Change starts from within

All change has to begin from within. Read below what an Anglican Bishop wrote in 1100 AD – apparently (the actual source is unknown). It is still true today. If you try to change your situation without making some change within yourself, however small, the chances are you will not succeed and you will still be dissatisfied. You cannot change other people, only yourself. It is only by changing yourself that you can hope to influence others and change situations.

Change
When I was young and free and my imagination had no limits,
I dreamed of changing the world.
As I grew older and wiser, I realised the world would not change.
And I decided to shorten my sights somewhat and change only my
country.
But it too seemed immovable.
As I entered my twilight years, in one last desperate attempt,
I sought to change only my family, those closest to me;
but alas they would have none of it.
And now here I lie in my death bed and realise,
perhaps for the first time, that if only I had changed myself first,
then by example I may have influenced my family and
with their encouragement and support I may have bettered my
country,
and who knows, I may have changed the world.

Doing a personal stocktake

As you are responsible for your own career development, it is important
to identify where and who exactly you are at the present time. Just like
a shop owner who evaluates his current stock before ordering new so he
does not over- or under-order, your personal stocktake allows you to
assess your current strengths and any areas which may need developing
if you are to move in a different direction. Until you know who and
where you are now, you will not know what or where to make the
changes that will make the difference to you. Self analysis helps you
decide where to make any changes, small or large. It is about defining
your present state (your current behaviours, thoughts and feelings)
before you can get to your desired state.

It is a bit like planning a garden. For example, to do it properly, it
would help to know:

● the state of the soil and what is needed to make it even better

● whether the garden is facing north or south, west or east

● where the plants are

● exactly what you have already in the garden.

If you do not do this, you risk plants struggling to grow in unsuitable
soil and possibly in the wrong location. So likewise, without an honest
appraisal of:

● the nature of your character

- your current strengths

- your likes and dislikes

- your current situation

you risk moving in an unsuitable and possibly wrong direction.

Being aware

So if you want to make some changes in your life, are you prepared to do some soul-searching, to consider first of all what kind of person you really are? Because it is only when you have some self-awareness that you can start to move forward purposefully – on purpose, with a purpose. If you do not do this, you could be doing yourself and others a disservice. If you are to be responsible for your own career development – in control of your own career – you will need this focus.

Many of us lack self-awareness. For instance, Tom thought he was someone people could rely on. He was always agreeing to meet people and yet rarely kept his appointments. When questioned about this, he always had a good excuse for not turning up. He could not understand when gradually he was no longer invited to social gatherings. As he had no understanding of his character, he could not begin to change his behaviour.

Starting the process

In order to gain some insight into your character, begin by completing Activity 1. Ask yourself how and where you demonstrate the character traits you have picked out. Then ask someone who knows you – a friend or a member of your family – to pick out the words that they think best describe you. Ask them to be as honest as they can be, as this is to help you. Compare your answers.

Did you agree on everything? If not, ask the other people why they chose the words they did and not all of the ones you did. Ask them for examples of when you demonstrated such personality traits. Discuss the reasons for them not agreeing with you on the ones you think you demonstrate. You may be surprised by some of the answers.

Jayne had always known she was assertive, but was shocked when friends described her as aggressive. She asked her friends to let her know immediately when they thought she was aggressive. Gradually she realised that it was her tone of voice which was making the difference between her intention and the message that was being received.

Think about any differences between your perception of your character and that of your friends and decide if there are any parts of your character you want to change in some way. Make a note of these changes and keep them to one side for referral as you move through the book.

Activity 1 – Describe yourself

Write down the words which you think best describe you. Then ask friends and/or family to do the same.

shy	adventurous	kind
logical	generous	serious
happy	sensitive	caring
talkative	easy going	punctual
determined	loyal	organised
worrier	critical	practical
hardworking	confident	lazy
polite	aloof	good with money

Add any other words you think may describe you, or change some of the words if necessary to suit your character better.

CELEBRATING YOUR ACHIEVEMENTS

Too often we concentrate on so-called mistakes and forget the many things we have achieved in our lives. It is also useful to remember that the little successes in life can be just as important as the big ones. Achievements can take many forms. What is an achievement for one person is not necessarily the same for another. This is demonstrated by the following examples of achievements in different spheres of our lives:

- **academic:** for example, gaining qualifications, from a degree to a unit of a first certificate; going back to study while at work or while raising a family; learning ten new words of a foreign language or being fluent in another language

- **personal:** for example, maintaining a positive attitude in the face of most challenges; deciding to change your life; overcoming a fear of water to learn to swim; taking up a new hobby or interest, or developing an existing one; being a good cook or simply making a 'mean' spaghetti bolognese; being a successful partner, parent, daughter/son, *etc*; maintaining a home for your family

- **work-related:** for example, typing, using a computer or having keyboard skills; being good at finance; being a successful negotiator; achieving sales targets
- **social:** for example, having a large circle of friends; helping others less fortunate; being a good listener; being a good neighbour
- **physical:** for example, being able to draw, paint, do DIY, sing, play a musical instrument, act, dance, write letters, stories or books; playing sport; keeping the garden looking good or encouraging just one plant to grow; climbing to the top of a hill or a mountain; maintaining a standard of fitness.

Identifying your own achievements

Are you beginning to understand exactly what form your achievements can take? Are you ready to identify what you have achieved to date in your life? You may need time to consider this. Take a piece of paper and something to write with. If you prefer to talk rather than write and if you have the resources to hand, have a tape recorder handy.

Brainstorming

This is where your unconscious mind is allowed to flow freely. Our minds are complex. The conscious mind is limited and only takes in a few pieces of information at a time. Its awareness is in the 'here and now'. To understand some of the power of the unconscious mind, just stand up and sit down. Now think about exactly what you had to do in order to do those two actions and imagine being aware of every muscle and bone in your body and each movement you make at all times. Most of what we do has to be done unconsciously, or we would take forever to make the slightest movement!

The unconscious mind therefore has power to be tapped. Brain-storming is a way of helping it to access as many unconscious thoughts as you wish. The trick is not to stop the flow so do not question anything you record. Just get it all on paper or tape as quickly as it pops into your mind. Help the stream of (un)consciousness by thinking in turn either about the categories listed above (academic, personal, work-related, social, physical) or about the various turning points or events in your life, such as:

- education
- relationships
- travel
- children

- employment/work
- house purchase
- making a home.

Talking to yourself
Now literally ask your unconscious to concentrate on all your successes and achievements to date, however little, in that particular area. Some people may feel a little foolish talking to themselves, but trust the process for now and see what results you get. It may be that you do not get anything immediately. If so, it may help to sleep on it.

Tricks of the mind
Distract your conscious mind by going for a walk, listening to some music, watching television or whatever you want. Unconscious thoughts often creep up on you when you least expect them. Have you ever forgotten something and remembered it in the middle of the night? Have you ever had a really good idea while relaxing in the bath? There is more on the power of the unconscious in Chapter 3.

Note down (either on paper or on the tape recorder) whatever thoughts come to mind. You can review it later. The important thing is to capture whatever your unconscious mind throws up.

Once you have a list, take a moment or two to examine it. Is it longer than you initially thought it might be? Allow yourself to feel proud of all that you have achieved and all that you are to achieve in the future, even though you may not know exactly what this will be yet. Keep this list somewhere safe to refer to, especially when you want to feel positive and have more confidence in yourself.

ASSESSING YOUR SKILLS AND EXPERIENCE

Many of us think we do not have any skills, or flounder if asked to think of any. This can be particularly true if you are unemployed or wanting to return to work, when confidence may be low. It can be a vicious circle: you experience a lack of confidence either because you cannot get a job or because you cannot imagine anyone wanting to employ you. Then because no one does employ you, you perpetuate the lack of confidence.

However, if you do not know what skills and experience you have (and we all have some), you have little chance of convincing others of them. You will also be unable to use them to their best advantage in whatever you decide to do with the rest of your life.

Defining what you have already

There are many ways of assessing your current skills and experience. One way is to look at the skills that were required of you in:

- the jobs you may have done

- your hobbies and interests

- your social and home life.

Remember too all the skills you may take for granted, such as being able to drive or exhibiting financial competence by managing the household budget. Many people are organisational wizards without recognising it. They are the ones who juggle a dozen or more priorities successfully, such as the children's activities, school runs, household chores, feeding a family, holding down a job, and so on.

Then look at the skills you may have been taught at school, such as literacy, numeracy, language, IT. Is your list getting longer?

Referring to your achievements

Another way of finding out what skills you have is to refer to your list of achievements. Ask yourself what skills you used to achieve what you did. For example, if you conquered a fear of water or heights, how did you do that? Was it through a determination to succeed? If so, this determination could be very useful in getting you what you want. Or had you set yourself a goal such as swimming or climbing a mountain, which meant you had to conquer your fear first? Goal-setting and perseverance in the face of obstacles are also very useful skills to have on board. What does being a good parent really mean? Think carefully about the reasons for your achievements (*how* did you do that? *what* is it that you did – specifically?) and you will soon have a long list of skills, based on your experiences.

Once you have identified your skills and experience, you will be able to build on them. You might also find that your self confidence is given a boost at the same time. Again, keep this list somewhere you can refer to it easily whenever you need that boost.

KNOWING YOUR RESOURCES

Before embarking on any project, it helps to know what resources you have available so that you can tap into them whenever necessary. There is little point in going it alone when help is available. What is meant by resources? They could include:

Materials

Many books, magazines, newspapers, tapes and computer software are now available on all manner of topics. Refer to the further reading section of this book.

People

How many people do you know who can help you? In what way? Is there someone who can support you, maybe by reminding you of what motivated you to read this book in the first place? Is there someone whom you can bounce ideas off? Someone else who can supply you with information? Make a list of everyone you know (friends, family, acquaintances, organisations, clubs) and in what way they can be a resource for you. You may be surprised at how willing people are to help you. Remember you are free to be someone else's resource in return.

Yourself

You have all the resources you need within you. You just have to draw them out. If you believe this, it means that anything is now possible. For instance, if you cannot do something, you might either believe that that is the end of the story or keep on trying in vain to do it, hitting the same old brick wall.

Believing that you have all the resources within you opens up the possibility of finding other ways to achieve what you want. It does not necessarily mean that you can instantly do everything just by having that belief. What it does mean is that we all have, for instance:

● the ability to be curious

● the desire to learn

● the will to ask questions

● the power to do something different

● the potential to find out information.

We can use these resources to research other possibilities. So if you cannot do something, maybe you know of someone else who can or maybe there is someone else who can teach you. It is about being creative or accessing the creative part of ourselves. It is also about being personally responsible for our own development.

GETTING STARTED

'Yesterday's history, tomorrow's a mystery, today's a gift which is why we call it the present.' Anon.

Once you have decided to make some changes in your life, it is important to identify the first step to be taken. Sometimes a new project can seem daunting just by its size. However, if the project is broken down into a series of smaller steps, then taking each step in turn becomes much easier. Remember a journey of a thousand miles started with just one step. This book started with the first word. Thinking about writing thousands of words can be scary; thinking about writing the first paragraph (and then the next and the next) is much less so. Breaking tasks down into smaller, manageable chunks is a good way of achieving goals more easily.

What will your first step be towards taking control of your career? What can you do now that will set you on the road to change? It may be deciding to read one chapter of this book or working through one exercise. It may be getting the support of family and friends. It will be different for each individual.

Motivating yourself

Write your reason for wanting to change and for reading this book on a piece of paper and stick it some place where you can see it often. This could act as motivation if necessary. Put your list of achievements, skills and experience where it will give your confidence a boost if necessary.

Planning the rest of your life

How much do you want to change things in your life? How much time are you willing to give to this? Depending on your answer, decide how you want to work through the book. Do you want to go through it a chapter at a time? Or does your lifestyle lend itself to you spending a set amount of time each day, each week or each month?

Unless you decide to do the exercises wholeheartedly, you could miss out on your dream career – is this something you really want to do? If not, how can you give yourself the time and space for this? Use your motivation for change as the carrot.

CASE STUDIES

Sheena learns about herself

Sheena wanted desperately to be liked and to be a part of the 'in' crowd. She had a busy life and was always rushing around. She tended to be very focused when she was working and did not always notice or even see or hear other people when they said 'hello' to her. If she did hear them, she quickly said 'hello' back and then got on with what she was doing. When she made time to stop and chat with other people, she often found they were not as friendly or as warm as she expected.

She did the self-assessment test and asked a couple of friends to choose the words that best described her. She could not believe that they had both chosen the word 'aloof' and not the word 'friendly'. She was simply not aware of the impression she was giving. Having asked her friends for examples of when she was aloof and unfriendly, she decided to make more of an effort to notice others around her and to respond to their smiles and greetings. It took a while to win back some people who had given up on her.

John recognises his true feelings

John was an accountant and earning a reasonable salary. He was well regarded and would almost certainly have been considered for promotion. However, one day John and some friends were playing a game of 'truth or dare'. He was asked: 'Did he enjoy his work?' This was something he had never considered before. It was like a kick in the stomach when he realised he could not truthfully say he enjoyed his work.

When he thought about what he did, he knew he was only going through the motions and that being an accountant was not how he wanted to spend the rest of his life. It certainly did not give him the buzz he needed. He did not yet know what he did want to do, but decided to start exploring the possibilities open to him by going to an adult guidance counsellor.

Trish identifies some skills

Trish was talking with some friends who were wondering how they could describe to other people how they spent their lives. They were fed up saying and almost believing that they were 'just a housewife'. They started joking about calling themselves a 'home maker', 'organisational and administrative expert', 'counsellor', 'mediator', 'negotiator', 'transport manager' and 'budget account manager'. Gradually Trish realised that they all had a range of skills, each one of which could be considered extremely useful. The one thing they were not was 'just a housewife'. In that moment Trish recognised that a seed of change had been sown.

CHECKLIST

1. Have you got paper and pens ready – and are you able and willing to set aside some time and space to work through this book?

2. Do you know why you want to make changes now? Write down your reasons and keep them somewhere handy as a motivator.

3. How self-aware are you now? Are there any bits of your character you want to change in some way, however small? Make a note of these for later use in the book.

4. Have you written your list of achievements?

5. Have you put this list somewhere you can find it easily whenever you need it?

6. Have you identified *all* your resources? Make a note of them as a reminder.

7. What is your starting point to be? What is the first step you will take on the road to taking control of your career?

2

Deciding What You Really Want

DECIDING WHICH CHANGES TO MAKE

When something in our lives is not working exactly as we want, do we always know the one thing to change that will make the difference? Often we do not and some people end up doing something drastic in a desperate attempt to find what it is they are missing. They change their jobs, move house or travel the world and yet nothing really changes. The reason is that they have not clearly identified the fundamental thing that will make the difference to their lives. They are simply changing one environment for another without solving the basic problem.

Getting to the bottom of the problem

It is a good idea to ascertain *exactly* what the problem is before you try to solve it. One way to do this is to get curious about yourself and the reason for your restlessness or unhappiness. Ask yourself lots of questions. For instance, if you are:

- **unhappy in your job:** is it the work you do? If the answer is yes, ask yourself more questions: is it *all* the work you do, or just parts of it? Is it the people you work with? If yes, again ask yourself: is it *all* or some of the people, your boss or some other person? Is it your attitude to your work that is the problem? Exactly what form does your unhappiness at work take?

- **wanting to do something more with your life:** does this mean earning money doing something useful or just doing something for fun? Or is it about showing the world what you are made of? Would doing some form of voluntary work be the answer? Do you need some ideas of different types of work? Exactly what does 'doing something more' mean for you?

- **wanting a job:** what is stopping you? Is it that there are no jobs available? Or is it that there are no jobs available for what you want to do? Are you not getting the opportunities you want or expect? Are you lacking in skills or in confidence, or in both? Do you need to earn a certain amount? Exactly what *is* stopping you from getting a job?

Arriving at some clarity

Your situation may or may not fit any of the above. However, asking yourself to be really specific about why you are reading this book in the first place could help you identify exactly what needs to change.

Only when you have begun to explore the specific problem can you begin to have clarity and start the process of solving it. For instance, if you discover that you are unhappy at work because of only one person, it may not be worthwhile changing your job. Another job might land you in exactly the same situation. It may be better to think about all the things that are good and important to you about your job and how you can enjoy it in spite of that person. In fact there may even be certain things you can do differently which would provoke a different response in that particular person. Remember:

> **If what you are doing is not working, do something different.**

This does not necessarily mean changing your job immediately if you are unhappy. What it does mean is taking an objective view and exploring what your options are. If you keep doing what you are doing, you are going to keep getting what you are getting. Doing something different might mean making major changes in your life or could mean tweaking a minor part of your life to major effect. It means looking at all aspects of a problem to see what would make the difference to you, however tiny.

For instance, if you keep being passed over for the promotion you believe you deserve, one course of action would be to change your job rather than to continue being disappointed. Another option would be to look at all the various aspects of your current job and ask yourself what a promotion would give you that you do not have already? If status or more money is the answer, how important are these to you? This is especially vital to answer, particularly if you are quite happy otherwise in what you do. If you decide that the work that you do now is actually more important to you than status or more money, you may be surprised at how unimportant that promotion suddenly becomes. What you have done differently is to change your attitude.

Changing your thoughts, behaviours and beliefs (covered in more detail in Chapters 5 and 6) can sometimes be all that is needed to change your life to the one you want to lead.

IDENTIFYING WHAT IS IMPORTANT

Think about what you are doing now and what is important to you about it. What do you do if you decide you like your work but not the people? Or if you like the people but not the work? How can you decide whether to do voluntary work or earn money from a job? Whether to go full-time, part-time or self-employed? The answer depends on what is important to you in life. Until you know that, it is pointless making any decisions or changes in your life. You would be making them without sufficient information and could risk still not having what you want.

What do you value most in life?

When asked this question, most people can come up with some answers, such as:

- family

- friends

- good standard of living

- health

- money

- knowledge

- security.

However, many people when pressed to prioritise those values find it difficult. Yet once we know what we value most, decisions become a lot easier to make. For example, Raj believed his values were health, love, friendship, helping others, adventure and money – in that order. He was offered a job with a very generous salary, doing something he wanted to do. It would mean him moving away from his friends and would leave him little time to keep fit, but in all other respects was just what he wanted. He turned it down with no regrets as it did not fit with what he valued in life. Money was low down on his list and so was not the motivating factor. Health and friendship were high up on the list and were two of the things he felt he would probably lose out on if he took the job.

Discovering your own values

There are many ways of discovering what is really important to you. One way is to think about what you would like people to say about you when you are dead. Do you want them to think of you as a good worker or a good friend, as someone who was always punctual or as someone who could be trusted? What would you like to read in your obituary? Once you know how you would like to be regarded, it becomes easier to live your life according to your values and to be in control of your career.

Another way to find out what your values are, is to try Activity 2. If you have difficulty choosing, look at each word and decide whether you could live without what it represents. Think about what each of these values gives you. For instance, if wealth is important to you, why? What does it give you? If you did not have it, what would it mean? Getting to the bottom of this helps clarify what is important to you.

Prioritising

If you choose more than ten words, take any one and compare it with another – which is more important to you? Prioritise them. Some people find this exercise not as easy as others, probably because it causes you to really think for maybe the first time about your life and what you value.

Once you have ten values, do the following:

- cross out two that are less important than the others

- of the eight that are left, cross out two that are less important than the others

- of the six that are left, cross out two that are less important than the others.

You now have your top four values. You can also prioritise these so that you have absolute clarity about what is important to you. It is very useful to do this, as it gives you a list of ranked criteria against which to measure your life, your work and your dreams. Is what you are doing now totally aligned with your values? If not, you now have some clues about what needs to change. For instance, if adventure comes top of your list and your job does not provide this, maybe you need to change jobs! Sorting out your values can also clarify why you are in certain situations. Someone who has money very low down on their list is less likely to be in a well-paid job than someone who has it higher up the list. The unconscious mind tends to give us what we say we want.

Regular and often

It is also important to do some kind of values exercise on a regular basis, because values do tend to change as individuals change over the years. What was important to you at the age of 20 may not be so important at the age of 40.

Activity 2 – What are your values?

From the list below, write down ten values that are most important to you in life. There will be many others not listed here. Feel free to add any values of your own that do not appear. Use this as a starter for ten!

Achievement	Adventure	Art	Balance
Challenge	Community	Creativity	Democracy
Effectiveness	Fame	Health	Helping others
Honesty	Independence	Family	Friendships
Growth	Knowledge	Laughter	Learning
Love	Loyalty	Money	Nature
Order	Pleasure	Power	Recognition
Relationships	Religion	Responsibility	Reward
Security	Self-respect	Serenity	Stability
Status	Success	Time	Truth
Wealth	Wisdom	?	?
?	?	?	?

CLARIFYING WHAT YOU WANT

Having worked out what your values are, you are one step nearer to clarifying what it is you want. Below are just some of the ways you can discover what your dream is.

When I grow up...

Remember when you were a child and anything seemed possible? Children are often very clear about what they want to be when they grow up. The television documentary 7-*Up* ably demonstrated this, showing a group of people at the age of seven articulating their hopes and dreams and then showing them at later stages of their lives, seeing who had achieved what they wanted. The seven-year-olds knew exactly what they wanted out of life.

Children appear to be unencumbered by concerns that affect adults. They give free rein to their imagination and often act out fantasy worlds. For some people, these childhood fantasies may provide the clue to where their future lies. What particular toys or activities fascinated you as a child? What was it that took all your attention and made you lose all sense of time? Take a moment or two to go back to that time and do not be too surprised at what thoughts come to you as you relive some magical childhood fantasies.

Thinking the impossible?

A lack of skills, qualifications, confidence or any number of things stop many of us from pursuing our dreams. Why not think the impossible?

What is your dream now? Is it still the one you had as a child and have not pursued? Or do you have a new one? One you only fantasise about and do not talk about for fear of being ridiculed? Now is the time to give yourself the luxury of bringing it into the open. As you are reading this now, you obviously have a desire to take control of your future, so why not make it the brightest one you can possibly imagine? What would you really love to do? Do you have a hobby, interest or special project that you would like to take up or pursue? A long-held ambition? Pretend you have a magic wand and can make anything happen – now.

Then take a piece of paper and either write or draw what your dream represents to you. Use coloured pens and, if you cannot draw, cut pictures out of a magazine. Let your creative mind go to town. Have fun with it. Children love 'cut and paste' activities and playing with coloured pens. Why should we be denied the same enjoyment just because we are adults?

Freeing your mind

What would you do if money was no object – if you were free to follow your dream? Would you continue the work you are doing now or would you do something different? Take as much time as you need to think about this.

Thinking about the present

Now consider your current situation, whether you are in a job or not.

● What things do you enjoy doing now?

● Is there anything you would rather do that you are not doing – yet?

● Is there anything missing in your life that would make a positive difference to you?

Going forward in time

Now you have some ideas about what you enjoy doing and maybe what you would rather do, it is fun to look forward and imagine what the future would be like doing what you really want to do. It is a bit like planning a journey. It helps to have a clear idea of your destination. Alice in *Alice in Wonderland* asked 'Would you tell me, please, which way I ought to go from here?' and was told 'That depends a good deal on where you want to get to'. There is of course no guarantee that you will get there on time and in exactly the place you want just by thinking about it. However, having some thoughts about your destination means that you can at least start moving towards it. You now know or can find out:

● where you are going

● how many roads lead there

● the direction of your journey.

You can start thinking about:

● how you will get there

● what you will need along the way

● who you want to go with you.

In the same way you can start to think about where you want to be in, say, five years' time. As with the journey, there is no guarantee of when and how you will arrive. You can, however, now begin to live your life on purpose. This is bound to increase your chances of arriving where you want, when you want. People like Richard Branson, James Dyson, Henry Ford, Bill Gates and other successful entrepreneurs and business people have got where they have by making plans and envisioning their future. Why not do the same? If you don't know where you are going, how will you know when you have got there?

As you become closer to knowing what you want to do with your life, you might find it helpful to share your thoughts with someone else. They can often offer a different perspective.

Daring to dream
Take a moment to focus on your values (what is important to you), your current life and all the things you would really like to do. Then try Activity 3. Time (at least ten minutes), peace and quiet make this exercise work particularly well.

What happened in that exercise? Did it give you any clarity on the direction in which you would like to move? Did you discover anything that would be useful to change in your current life if you are to get what you want from life? If not, it may help to do the exercise again, now you know what to do. Relax even more and trust your unconscious mind to do the work for you.

Like your values, it is useful to review any long-term plan from time to time. Things happen that cause us to change our views. Ask yourself if you still want to go in a particular direction or pursue another opportunity that has opened up somewhere else. Continue to be flexible, both in your thoughts and behaviour, as well as in your actions.

Positive thinking
Allow yourself to think only of the possibility of achieving your dream; this is not the time or place for 'yes, but...'. The next section looks at the implications of all this and Chapter 8 looks at how to overcome any obstacles to your goal. So suspend your disbelief for now. Put all thoughts of non-achievement and impossibility to one side – you can have them back later if you really want them!

Now you have some type of record of your dream, be sure to keep it safe.

RECOGNISING THE IMPLICATIONS

So what does it mean to have a dream or some notion of where you would like to be in the future? It means that you are giving yourself the chance of having what you want. Now you have some idea of what you want from life, it may be worth thinking about two important questions:

Activity 3 – Daring to dream

You can do this by simply reading and then doing, or you could tape the words and play them back to yourself, so that you can enter fully into the experience by closing your eyes and allowing your unconscious mind to conjure up the images that present themselves. If you choose to tape the words, put in plenty of pauses between the questions so that you give yourself time to process (to think about) the question and explore what it means. You may even want to record your answers in some way, as a reminder.

Close your eyes and take a couple of deep, relaxing breaths. Now consider what your life would be like if it continued exactly as it is now for the next, say, five years, with nothing changing. Imagine yourself five years older. View your future as though you were living it now, through your own eyes, as if you were looking out of them. Where are you? What exactly are you doing? Who or what do you see around you? Are there any sounds? How does it feel? Is it somewhere pleasant, unpleasant, fantastic or horrible?

Open your eyes and take a moment to let any images that formed disappear. Stand up, move around and look around you now as you are in the present. Maybe look outside, just to make sure you are not still in the previous picture.

Now close your eyes and do the same as before, breathing in deeply and letting your breath out gently once or twice. Project yourself, say, five years hence. This time, imagine that your life is exactly as you want it. Remember to look through your own eyes. Where are you now? What exactly are you doing? Who can you see? What can you hear? And what do you feel now? Is the feeling any different to the time before?

Open your eyes and let the images drift away. Again, move around so you are fully back in the here and now. You may want to write down quickly any thoughts or ideas, however fantastic, that came to mind during the exercise.

NB. If you find five years is too far away for you to contemplate, try this exercise with a different timescale – one that would work for you. Remember, it is your life, so you get to choose how to plan it. This is just a guideline.

1.   What would happen if you got what you wanted?

2.   What would happen if you didn't?

It is important to think through all the implications. Remember King Midas and his touch of gold? He got what he thought he wanted and was surprised when literally everything he touched turned to gold. How many people say they want to win the Lottery and yet sudden wealth is not always a good thing. Some National Lottery winners who thought they wanted millions of pounds were surprised when their lives changed completely and not always for the better. Maybe they had not considered any negative effects of winning a fortune and were not prepared. Make sure you do not make the same mistake and that you really do want what you say you do.

Think about implications not only for you and your well-being but also for anyone close to you. Having what you want often means that other people are also affected by your actions. It is useful to consider exactly what this would mean for them.

You may want to write down your answers to the questions so that you can refer to them as and when you need to.

MOTIVATING YOURSELF

How serious are you about wanting to change? What are you willing to do to make it happen? Could you take risks, overcome obstacles, follow your dream no matter what? Are you ready to take control of your own career?

Many people set goals or make New Year resolutions and fail to keep them. One reason for this could be that there is not enough motivation. Motivation has to be strong enough to override any obstacles, such as 'not enough time', a common one blamed for not putting something into practice. There are various actions you can take to remind you of your motivation to take responsibility for your own life:

● Write down the **reason you want to change** and, even more importantly, the benefits that change will give you. Keep this somewhere prominent. For example, some people, when they are slimming, paste a picture of themselves on the fridge door, to remind themselves either of what they want to look like or what they are moving away from. Where would be the most useful place for you to put your reminder? And what form should it take?

- **Tell someone else about your plans** and ask them to support you by reminding you of your motivation for doing this. They could do this on a regular basis, either on the telephone or face to face. You are in control so you set the parameters. How often would you need or want someone to ask 'how are you doing?'. Do you want them to pat you on the back for progress or do you need them to keep on at you to move forward? What works best for you in terms of motivation?

- There may be someone else going through a similar situation to you. Maybe you could offer each other **mutual support**. Sharing problems and information can be very motivating. Some people also like a sense of competition to motivate themselves: for example, could you agree on a certain date by which you and your friend will have achieved something, with prizes for the person who gets there first?

- It is important to be in the **right frame of mind** to make change. If you are feeling negative, you will probably not be as imaginative or as purposeful as you might be if you were in a more positive mood. Some people get themselves 'into the mood' by writing or saying words of encouragement to themselves or recording them on tape and playing them back. Could this work for you? See the example given in Activity 4 for motivating someone to write creatively. Can you write something that would be equally meaningful for you? Could you adapt what is written to suit your circumstances? And if you cannot, do you know someone else who could. Remember – you have all the resources within you!

CASE STUDIES

Beth reassesses her values

Beth worked for an international oil company. She was earning an excellent salary with many perks, such as subsidised overseas travel, theatre and cinema tickets. Although she knew she was lucky, she also felt there was something missing in her life. She began to look at other careers, by going to the library and reading through careers books. The ones that interested her were the ones categorised as 'caring careers' – social work, teaching, careers advice. She realised that what was missing in her current job was making a direct contribution to other people. She decided to retrain as a teacher. It was hard to give up the money, to leave her colleagues and the job she knew for the unknown, but she realised that it *felt* right.

Activity 4 – Words to motivate

This text is for a writer. Note the use of the word 'right' throughout which the mind hears also as 'write', prompting the unconscious mind to do exactly this – write! Can you change any of the underlined words to meet your own specific purpose?

'Fortunately I know you know how much more easily creative minds flow when you slow down your conscious mind and begin to allow your unconscious mind to tap into the creativity and all the many other resources you have easily accessible within you...

and as you're sitting in your chair, feeling your feet on the floor and hearing the sounds outside and inside in the room while looking forward to the pleasures of the day ahead, begin to notice just how important it is to be still and calm, and take a moment or two to contemplate, becoming more focused with every gentle breath you take, breathing energy in from your toes *right* up to your head, and letting any tension seep out...

while the deep sense of well-being you have continues to create good feelings, powerful feelings, *right* through your whole body and I wonder how soon it will be before you realise how enjoyable it is to draw pictures in people's minds from the inspiring and interesting words that flow easily and quickly from you like water tumbling down a waterfall which starts *right* at the beginning and cannot help but be motivated to flow *right* to an exciting and bubbling end ready to continue its flowing journey elsewhere ...

while you're in this state know that you can be *right* in it wherever you are and whenever you want as you become once more aware of your breathing and of the sights and sounds in the room and focus on the day ahead of you now as with real energy and a sense of purpose you are ready to begin. *Right* NOW.'

Jez does some long-term planning

Jez had lived in London for nearly ten years and had toyed with the idea of leaving for the past few years. He wanted to move back to the south of England where his family was. Every New Year he would make the same resolution – 'must look for jobs down south' and every year he would do nothing to make that happen. So one year he decided to actually put a date on when he wanted to move. He decided on April twelve months hence. He told all his friends that he would be leaving London next April. Having a date to work towards really spurred him into action. With that as his focus, he actually started job searching and asked his father to send him the local paper regularly. In April of the following year he had an interview for a new job and moved down south three months later.

Toni learns to be flexible

Toni had tried so hard to get a job. She had sent off hundreds of application forms and yet had not been asked to one interview. She kept sending off the forms and becoming more depressed as rejection slips continued to come through the letter box. A friend suggested that maybe she needed to change tactics as what she was doing was obviously not working. So Toni asked for advice from a careers adviser on how to fill in her application forms and made some changes as a result. She sent off for two jobs and still did not make it to the interview stage. So she changed something else in the forms and tried again. On the fourth attempt she was invited to her first interview.

CHECKLIST

1. Do you know the specific reasons why you want to make a change?

2. What are your values? Can you say what your top four are?

3. Is your life aligned with your values now?

4. What is the one thing that would make a difference to you now, all things being possible?

5. Do you know where you will be in five years' time?

6. Have you noted in some way what your dream is?

7. What would happen if you got what you wanted?

8. What would happen if you didn't?

9. What motivation strategies do you need in place to make some changes?

3

Training Your Mind

'If you set your mind to it, you can accomplish anything.'

Do these words sound familiar? Has anyone ever said them to you before? Do you really believe it or think it is only true for some people? This is the chapter where you can experiment in using your imagination and getting your mind, your conscious and unconscious mind, on your side in your goal-setting. Too often people set goals half-heartedly without engaging their whole mind in the process and then wonder why they are not achieving what they set out to do. The secret is to feed your unconscious with the appropriate messages so that it works for you in the way you want it to.

DARING TO GO FOR IT

You have now begun the process of creating an irresistible and compelling future for yourself. However unclear it may be at the moment, capture its essence somehow (by a drawing, symbol or writing) and clarity will come later – particularly if you ask your unconscious mind. Remember your unconscious mind is part of you and wants to work for you, so get it on board!

Stating your goal positively

The brain does not recognise the difference between a negative and a positive statement. If it is told not to think of something or not to do something, what happens? Remember being told as a child 'don't touch' or Basil Fawlty saying 'don't mention the war'? The result was in the first case always touching what you were told not to as a child and in the second everyone mentioning the war whenever they opened their mouths.

The brain has to think of what it wants to avoid before it can avoid it. This could be one reason why it is so hard to diet because your brain continually thinks about food! It is therefore better to express whatever you want positively – for example, a slimmer body – so you can be more sure of achieving it. It is also important to choose a goal which is fully

Activity 5 – 8-step process to arrive at your goal

1. What do you want? **State it in the positive**. For instance, if you say 'I don't want a full-time job', ask yourself what you would rather have; if you say 'I don't want to be a housewife all my life', ask yourself what you would rather be; if you say 'I don't want to stay here forever', ask yourself where you would rather be. Do not go on to the second step until you have stated what you want rather than what you do not want. Simply by identifying what you want, you are increasing the probability of getting it.

2. How will you know when you have it? **What will you see, hear and feel – specifically?** For example, Jade's goal is to have a job within six months, so he sees himself in an office, sees himself receiving an employment contract, hears voices around him welcoming him to the company, hears himself saying 'well done, you made it!', feels that warm, contented feeling of happiness mixed with the flutterings of anticipation. Are you getting the picture? Do whatever works for you. You may also want to set a time frame as Jade did.

3. **What are the implications of having what you want?** How will it affect you? Will it affect anyone else? Is it still OK to have what you want? For instance, if you want to go back to work, what effect will that have on your family? Can you talk to and get the support from your family that may be required? Ask yourself 'If I could have the result I want now, would I take it?' and notice your response. If you say 'yes' with a slight hesitation, or there is a 'but' creeping in after the 'yes', this probably means that your goal needs refining in some way. Maybe it is too big or too small (see step 4 below), or maybe a time frame would be helpful. You decide and check out your amended goal each time against all these steps.

4. **Is your goal too big or too little?** If it is too big, you might find it too daunting even to get started on it. Chapter 1 referred to a journey of a thousand miles starting with just one step. The secret is to break it into small manageable steps, with each step being an individual goal. If your goal is too little, it may not be big

Activity 5 – continued

enough to motivate you to get started. In this case, think about what achieving it would really give you. What difference would it make to your life? For instance, taking one step on a journey would get you closer to your destination. Your destination then becomes the real motivating factor, not the first step. Knowing this may give your first step the importance it needs for you to make it.

5. **What part will you play** in achieving this goal? Is it in your control or someone else's? If it is not primarily in your control, it will be difficult to achieve because you are then relying on other people. If this is the case, think about your goal in terms of what *you* can do to change things. Remember the Anglican Bishop's alleged words at the beginning of the book?

6. **What resources do you need** to achieve your goal? What do you have already? Think not only about material resources, but about people who can help you and about which of your own resources would be useful, such as confidence, specific skills, clarity, creativity, energy, and so on.

7. Is there anything you may do that could **sabotage** your chances of arriving at your goal? For instance, is there ever a little voice inside you that says 'oh, why bother, it'll never work' or 'I'll do that tomorrow, I have other important things to do right now'? If so, think now about how you can overcome any negative thoughts or procrastination. It may be that you need to have your motivation strategies well in place before you begin (refer back to the last chapter).

8. **What action can you take now,** will you take now, to start the journey towards your goal? It may be a simple thing, such as making time in your diary to do certain things or buying a particular national newspaper on a regular basis to look for jobs; or it may be bigger, such as filling in the application form you have had for ages or talking to your boss about changing some of your duties.

thought through and perfectly achievable. Activity 5 sets out an eight step process which, if followed properly and comprehensively, will ensure you achieve your goals from now on. By expressing your goal so clearly, you are giving your unconscious mind all the information it needs to help you successfully work towards achieving it.

Having something to aim for

Viktor Frankl was a psychiatrist in Vienna before World War II. He was also one of the few who survived Auschwitz. He did so because he believed he still had something significant yet to do. In *Man's Search for Meaning*, he tells of how he 'forced his thoughts to turn' from the suffering and futility of life all around him and saw himself in the future, observing the sufferings 'as if now of the past'. He set himself the goals of:

- surviving

- using his medical skills to alleviate as much suffering as possible in Auschwitz

- trying to learn something from his experiences.

He succeeded in all three. Many stronger, younger and healthier people did not survive. Maybe they did not have clear goals. We will never know, but we do know that Frankl had goals and that he survived. His is an inspiring tale of a man overcoming insurmountable odds and giving meaning to his life. If he can do that in the most difficult of circumstances, how much can you do in your life now?

What's stopping you?

Even if you have worked through the process outlined in Activity 5, you may not believe that by doing this you can have what you want. There may still be perceived obstacles in your way, such as your age, lack of resources (such as finance, skills, qualifications, confidence) or any other personal circumstance that you see as an barrier. Overcoming such obstacles is covered in detail in a later chapter, but for the time being, write down a list of why you *can* do what you want, not why you cannot. Keep that handy for reference.

DREAMING CREATIVELY

If as a child you were often told that daydreaming was not a worthwhile activity, it is likely that you eventually lost the habit of doing this. It is in fact an extremely useful thing to do, as it allows the mind free rein to roam. The best ideas are often those that come when you least expect them to. It is possible to tap this source and use it to its best advantage. Give yourself permission to daydream. Be surprised at what thoughts you conjure up.

Visualising what you want

There is nothing in this world that was not imagined first. Everything around you was created first in someone's mind. It is thanks to the fertile imagination of designers, engineers, inventors, artists, scientists and other visionaries that we can not only fly but reach the moon. Who would have thought it? Someone did.

It is possible to structure your daydreams. You can do this by:

● getting yourself into a **relaxed state** (make sure the phone is turned off and that you will not be disturbed for ten minutes or so). Close your eyes and take a few deep, calming breaths in and out.

● **visualising what you want.** Actually create an image in your mind's eye. See it through your own eyes – looking out through your eyes.

● **engaging all your senses fully.** Give the image its full colour. Make the colours bright and focused. The bigger the picture, the more real it usually becomes. Add in any sounds, tastes or smells if appropriate. Really feel as though you are there in the present, receiving whatever it is you want. What feelings does that evoke in you?

Do this as many times as you want until you receive what you want. It can be a powerful exercise and so it helps if you are very explicit in your visualisation. Sometimes the universe gives you the essence of what you want, for example, if you visualised a car, you may not become the owner of one but may find someone else who has one and is willing to give you lifts. Notice what it is you receive. You may be surprised. Be prepared to be patient. If you do not get what you want when you want, it may be because it is not the right time – yet.

Guided visualisation

This is a technique that is sometimes used in yoga relaxation. Its aim is to distract the conscious mind with a story or metaphor. The unconscious mind then responds to the messages given by the metaphor on a different, deeper level. This is a way of reaching the unconscious mind directly. The use of the word 'right' in Activity 4 (Chapter 2) is an example of this. Hypnosis also uses this technique of distracting the conscious mind to give messages to the unconscious.

Activity 6 – Guided visualisation

You may want to record this on to tape and play it so that you can enter fully into the experience. If you do not have access to a tape recorder, you could ask a friend to read it to you and then you reciprocate, or you could read it through a couple of times and then remember it as you relax and close your eyes. However you decide to do it, make sure you give your mind enough time to process the information you are feeding it. Read more slowly than you would normally. Put in pauses, especially where marked.

Make sure you will not be disturbed for ten minutes. Get comfortable and ensure you are warm enough, Now close your eyes and take a long, deep breath in and as you breathe out, let all tension leave your body. Do this twice more.

PAUSE

Imagine you are going for a country walk. It is a warm sunny day, you can hear birds singing and see wild flowers in the hedgerows. You are feeling on top of the world and even hum a tune in your head. Ahead of you is a field. You go through the gate and see a meadow in front of you. The field is bordered by thick hedges, one of which has a stile halfway along. You walk through the long grass, stopping every now and then to pick a daisy or a buttercup. The stile leads into the most beautiful rose garden you have ever seen. The smell is almost overpowering. You cannot resist entering. One rose in particular draws you to it. You go right up to it, smell its perfume and as you look down, it unfurls to reveal an image of you inside.

PAUSE

You leave the field by the same stile, walking back the way you came. You keep with you the image you saw in the rose as you slowly come back to full consciousness by opening your eyes.

Now write down or record in some other appropriate way what the exercise revealed to you. What colour was your rose? Was it fully formed, a bud, at its peak or ready to drop its petals? Was its stem thorny? What did you look like? Happy or sad? You may find that only some of this makes any sense to you at first. If this is the case, allow your unconscious mind to work on it and it will give you more clarity when you are ready to receive it.

The good thing is that your unconscious mind will not allow you to do anything that is against your higher good, *ie* your values and ethics (provided you know what these are!). Remember, it is on your side. If you want to experience its effects, try the guided visualisation in Activity 6.

USING YOUR INTUITION

How often do you have a 'gut feeling' that something is right or wrong? How often do you trust it? It is important to recognise what your body is telling you. It is being guided by your unconscious mind, which is on your side, provided you give it the right messages!

An easy way to recognise a good or bad feeling is to remember a time when you just knew something was right or wrong and your instinct, your intuition, turned out to be true. Take a moment now to think back to a situation (*eg* a job offer, a new house, a new relationship) where you knew it was the right thing to accept and where it all turned out well for you. Imagine yourself as you are, experiencing that feeling now – see what you saw, hear what you heard and feel what you felt back then as if you are feeling it now. Remember that feeling – where was it? What exactly was it like? Could you recognise it again?

Now do the same for something that you knew would not work out and, as it happened, you were right (*eg* job offer, relationship). Remember that feeling. How different is it to the other feeling? Could you recognise it again?

You now have at your disposal an ability to interpret your instinct. You can test it by seeing if you can evoke either feeling, good or bad, just by being. If they are true 'gut' feelings, you will not be able to reproduce them at will. They are there as your guides.

ENCOURAGING YOURSELF

Using the power of the unconscious

It is possible to encourage yourself by giving yourself treats for targets reached, for example, a coffee break if you get a report finished, some new clothes if you reach a certain weight, a present if you pass an examination. There are also other, less expensive ways to give yourself encouragement. The unconscious mind, as noted above, responds to the messages we give it. So why not give it positive messages, by thinking such thoughts as 'I am doing well', 'I have so many ideas', 'I am reaching my goal', 'I have such energy'? It is important to put these messages in the present tense, so that you trick the unconscious into believing they are already true. It will then do whatever is necessary to support that belief.

Changing the voice inside

Many of us admit to having a little voice inside which gives us messages, not always ones we want to hear. This is the voice that says things like 'you must be joking, you can't do that!', 'come on, get a move on, why don't you', 'I wish I could do that but...', 'I always get it wrong', 'I'll never get this finished on time', 'I'm so tired'. Does this sound familiar at all?

The way to get round these negative messages is to remember that it is your head we are talking about. You are free to change those messages any time you want. Next time you hear yourself saying 'I can't...' or 'I will never...', or anything else unhelpful, change it to something you do want to hear. Change the tone of voice if that helps. Keep doing this until it becomes more natural to you and you do not need to change anything, because it is all positive. Notice what difference it makes to you.

Using affirmations

As well as having the voice inside your head on your side, it is also a good thing to express thoughts out loud. It somehow makes them even more real. It is the same when we write things down. It is as if we are giving our unconscious mind a definite message for it to act upon. Many people use affirmations (positive statements that something is already happening) to help them achieve what they want. Some people say you do not even have to believe the statements for them to work; others think they work better if they are backed up by a firm belief. Experiment and see what works for you.

See Activity 7 for examples of affirmations and consider which ones you would like for yourself, maybe filling in the gaps. For them to work properly, they need to be stated positively and in the present tense. Once you have some, either for your work or your personal life, write them down and practise saying them out loud. It is often best if you are alone when you do this, or others might think you are exhibiting the first signs of madness!

Some people believe that looking in a mirror as you say them tends to give them even more potency. It may be something to do with seeing and believing or engaging more than one of your senses. By writing affirmations down, saying them and looking at yourself, you are already using three of your senses. The more senses you use, the stronger the message and the learning.

Activity 7 – Affirmations

I have all the resources I need within me.

I am attracting riches towards me.

I am healthy (*particularly useful when you have a cold!*).

All is well in my world.

I am a creative person.

I am happy and fulfilled in what I do.

I always have everything I need.

I am…

I have…

I love…

Acting as if it were true

Another powerful technique involves tricking the mind into believing that something is true. For instance, if you believe you lack confidence, act as if you had it. There may have been a time when you were confident or times when you are confident, depending on the situation. If this is so, remember the experience – how did you look and sound and what feelings did that evoke in you?

If you believe you have never been confident, look around you at confident people, see how they behave, notice what they do that is different to you. Look especially at their posture, how they hold themselves. Listen to the way they speak. Watch the way they move. Imitate them. Notice how your feelings change as your behaviour changes. This method of acting 'as if' can be a source of great encouragement and give you a boost whenever you need it.

Mixing with the right people

Some people have the knack of bursting other people's bubbles just by their attitude. If they are having a bad day, week, month or year, they want others to buy into their view of the world. Before you know it, you are sharing their negative outlook on life. Your mind responds to whatever it is fed. If you mix with negative minded people, you will almost certainly begin feeling negative too. How much better to surround yourself with people who will bring out the best in you and who have a positive view of the world. Who do you want in your corner? It is your choice. So take control of your life.

HAVING SOME FUN

Once you have understood the art of creative visualisation and its possibilities, you may want to practise on things that do not have 'life and death' importance. For instance, many people visualise parking spaces just where they want them! Others imagine journeys without any hold-ups. What do you want to visualise and make happen?

If someone is not having a good day, they say something along the lines of 'I'm having a bad hair day' or 'I'm having one of those days (when nothing goes right)' or even 'I just got out of the wrong side of bed today'. Why not decide instead to treat yourself to:

● a good hair day?

● a day when just everything goes right?

● a good day because you got out of the *right* side of bed?

Notice how different your expectations and experiences are if you change your thought patterns.

CASE STUDIES

Winning against all odds

A newspaper (*The Times* 28.5.98) reported that Tom Whittaker had successfully climbed Everest at the age of 49. It was his third attempt. Climbing Everest at any age is remarkable and the older we get the more remarkable it is. It is therefore even more surprising to learn that Tom is a one footed amputee, having lost his right foot in a car accident. A colleague said 'his dream has become reality'. What powerful vision did he create for himself before starting off on his climb? Could he have done this without training his mind as well as his body?

Take any athlete

Successful athletes and sports people achieve their goals by visualising them first. Sally Gunnell sees herself breaking the winner's tape before any race. The success of a tennis player can sometimes depend on how well they see the ball hitting the ground exactly where they want it to before serving. Many athletes also use a lot of self encouragement as they perform, whether it's slapping their thighs, talking to themselves out loud or using certain gestures to goad themselves on.

CHECKLIST

1. Write down your goal by following the 8-step process (Activity 5).

2. Give yourself permission to daydream. Notice what new ideas you have as you do this.

3. Are you able to use your 'gut' instinct to recognise good or bad decisions?

4. Write out some powerful affirmations. Say them out loud at least twice a day, once on waking and once before sleeping.

5. Surround yourself with people who are positive.

6. Act as if you had certain strengths. Notice how your behaviour changes your thoughts and vice versa. The body and mind are connected!

7. Give your unconscious mind positive messages. Treat yourself to a good hair day.

4

Recognising What Skills You Need

KNOWING WHAT IS WANTED IN THE WORKPLACE

Identifying the future skill requirements

There are highly marketable skills such as language, financial, organisational, writing, keyboard or expertise in IT which are useful for any industry. There are also skills which are specific to certain occupational areas, such as engineering, planning, accountancy, medicine, surveying, sales and so on. Which marketable and job-specific skills do you have?

It is always hard to predict which specific skills are going to be needed in the future. It can depend very much on the country's or even the world's economy. There are also some useful publications such as *Labour Market and Skills Trends,* which is produced annually by the Skills and Enterprise Network on behalf of the DfEE. It gives information about the changing nature of jobs, employment prospects and future employment trends. A copy may be available for reference:

- in your local careers service company

- in your local TEC/LEC

- in your local Business Link

- if you have access to the Internet on
  http://www. open. gov.uk/dfee/skillnet/senhome.htm.

It is also possible to get some idea of what is happening in the labour market and what employers are looking for by scanning the job advertisements, reading the business section of newspapers or looking at Jobcentre vacancies.

Making predictions

Some predictions are easier to make than others. For example, it is likely that the demand for IT skills will continue even after the year 2000 problem (the millennium computer bug) is solved, given the rapid and constant changes occurring in hardware and software. There are many opportunities currently for IT specialists, although basic IT skills are now regarded by employers as a key skill rather than a vocationally specific one.

There does also seem to be a continuing movement towards a more service-orientated economy. With a greater focus on customer care and service, people who have the ability to communicate well, to handle all kinds of situations and who have good interpersonal and social skills will always be in demand.

Greater skill range
Employers are looking for people with a broader spread of skills than ever before. Employees are often expected now to cover a wider range of tasks and to have a greater depth of knowledge within their particular skill areas. Although job-specific skills are obviously still vital, they can often be learnt or acquired more easily than generic skills such as teamwork, oral, organisational, listening, reasoning and written skills. Personal values and qualities are also important, such as motivation, discipline, leadership and initiative. These can be useful whether you are employed, unemployed or self-employed.

Transferring skills
Many skills which are useful in one area can be as equally useful in another. For instance:

- **Bar work** requires you to work under pressure and occasionally deal with difficult customers. Working effectively under pressure is a valuable skill for almost any job. Employers, particularly in the retail and service sectors, would welcome someone with the ability to deal with difficult customers.

- Playing **team sports** such as cricket, football, netball or hockey requires teamwork, a skill employers are emphasising more and more as important.

- **Office work** develops skills valid in any other job, including organisational and interpersonal skills.

- Demonstrating **initiative**, completing projects on time and managing staff are all qualities useful in any line of work.

Which skills of yours are transferable to other areas of work? Take a moment or two to write out a list now. Look at all the ones mentioned above and identify where and how you demonstrated them. It is always important to provide evidence of ability and achievement to employers. Think about all areas of your life, not just those of employment. What skills do you demonstrate in your social or home life? Keep the list handy as it could act as a confidence booster, reminding you of how skilled you already are, and could also be used in preparation for future employment opportunities.

Marketing yourself

Whether you are trying to get support from someone for your ideas, a loan from a bank to set up in business, or a job, the important thing is how you are perceived – how you sell yourself. Enthusiasm, commitment and a willingness to learn count for a lot and have even been known to make up for many shortcomings and lack of specific skills. As stated above, some skills are easier to acquire than personal qualities.

Preparing for interview

According to research, the questions most asked by job interviewers relate to how well you know yourself and whether you have set goals in your personal and working life. For instance, questions include some of the following:

● What have you done that shows initiative in your career?

● What does teamwork mean to you?

● What have you learned from jobs you have held?

● What do you want to be doing five years from now?

● What is your ambition?

● What is your major weakness?

How well can you answer these questions now? It is a good idea to think about these now before you have the pressure of an interview to prepare for. By doing some thinking now, you can save time in the future. Answers to these and other questions will be useful whether you are going for job interviews or not, as they will give clarity to your goals.

Getting specific help with CVs

CVs are not always easy to get right. It can sometimes be useful to ask for help from an independent source, such as a careers consultant or careers service company. Alternatively, do you know of anyone who deals with recruitment and selection? They may be willing to look at your CV and give you a second opinion. There are also many excellent books, available from public libraries or bookshops, on writing a good CV.

Part of the difficulty in writing the perfect CV is that it does not exist. Even experts differ about its format, content and length. This is because it means different things to different people. We are all unique and have our own individual view of the world. However, even accepting this premise, there are some basic rules which are generally agreed to be common to all CVs:

- Keep it **short** (1–2 A4 pages maximum); concise and well-organised CVs do tend to work better than long, rambling ones, because recruiters usually have only a small amount of time to sift through a pile of applications.

- Make it **relevant** to the job for which you are applying.

- Give evidence of your skills and achievements – give examples of when you demonstrate(d) them.

- Type it on **good quality paper** and ask someone to proofread it. It can often be hard to notice your own mistakes.

- Take a **copy**, so you can remember what you wrote!

- If it is not successful in getting you interviews, look at ways of changing it.

ACKNOWLEDGING WHAT YOU HAVE ALREADY

Look back to the section on skills above. Which skills do you have already that would benefit you in your quest to take charge of your career? There are many skills that people have and take for granted. How many do you have which you had not realised? For example, some parents are excellent communicators, negotiators and organisers. Ask your family and friends for their opinion on your skills. Write them down and congratulate yourself at the same time.

Do you have a skill, ability, hobby or interest that could already earn you some money or which could be developed easily?

TRAINING YOURSELF

Taking responsibility

It can sometimes be useful to consider yourself the Managing Director of your own company – Myself Incorporated. Think of anyone you work for as your customers. It is now your responsibility to ensure you give the customers what they want. How can you ensure your training and skills are adequate to do this?

Gaining new skills or updating the skills you have

It is important to take any opportunity to widen your skills. When did you last do some training or take an evening class for your own benefit? It can sometimes be useful to decide to learn something new at least once a year. What new skills could you learn or would you like to learn? Many colleges of further education offer a range of low cost day and evening classes where you can learn anything from car maintenance to computer skills. Ask for a prospectus and enjoy finding a class to suit you.

Deciding what you need or want to learn and taking steps to learn it is a sign of being in control of your life. Make sure you keep track of the skills you are developing by adding them to your ever-growing list.

Going for it no matter what

There may be some tasks you find daunting at first. For instance, some people do not relish the thought of going back to college. There may be many reasons for this, such as previous experiences of education or a lack of confidence. If this is true of you, it may be helpful to think first about the benefits college could give you, such as new skills, new friends and new experiences.

Accessing education

If you have bad memories of education, that is all they are – memories. Things are different now. You are older and motivated to learn. Colleges welcome adult learners. It is also possible to go on to higher education, even if you do not yet have the necessary entry qualifications, by taking an 'access course'. These courses are designed for anyone over the age of 17 and are usually one year in duration. Some are designed for entry to specific degrees while others are of a more general nature. Ask at your local college for details.

If you are feeling timid about going back to education on your own, do you have a friend who also wants to learn? It is often easier to go to college with someone, even if you are going to different classes in the same college. Look at the section on page 53 'Increasing your confidence' and also refer back to Chapter 3, the section on 'Encouraging Yourself' which gives tips on how to increase your confidence.

Alternatively, consider distance learning. There may be distance learning packages offered by colleges which may be relevant to your training needs and which may suit you better than attending a college. Ask at your local college for details.

Learning by mistakes

People are often fearful of learning something new in case they fail. Believing that 'there is no failure only feedback' means that whatever happens, we learn from it and therefore mistakes are welcomed because they teach us something (if only another way not to do something!). Why not give yourself permission to make as many mistakes as you can? The key is to learn from them.

Thomas Edison is often cited as an example of someone who decided to learn through failure. Even after thousands of failed attempts to make the electric light bulb he carried on. He said 'I am not discouraged, because every wrong attempt discarded is another step forward'.

Learning from work

Look at how to gain experience and skills together (see page 54 about gaining experience), through voluntary work or paid work (temporary, casual). Any work is useful, even if you decide never to do a particular type of work again, as it is evidence of what you are capable of. It may also help you decide whether you like a certain job or activity.

If you feel stuck in a job and want to learn new skills, why not change jobs? Have not only new experiences but develop new skills as well. Be the first to learn anything new, such as IT. Help to plan and initiate change. Explore the possibility of having on-the-job or off-the-job training.

Increasing your confidence

Lack of confidence is one of the most common reasons for many people not getting back into the workplace, not getting a job in the first place or not setting out on a new venture, whatever it might be.

One way to improve your confidence is to look at all the things you do well rather than focusing on the things you do not. People lacking in confidence are often very hard on themselves. For example, Nerys started having swimming lessons less than a year ago. She can now swim 75 lengths in 45 minutes and yet considers herself a failure because other people in the class can do more. How much better to measure herself against her own progress, not against other people's. Begin to note and celebrate your successes.

Other ways to have more confidence in yourself include:

● Studying people who are confident, imitating what they do, see, hear and feel.

● Acting as if you are confident until you actually feel it.

- Experiencing the situation where you want to be more confident in advance, by role playing or rehearsing it either with a friend or on your own.

- Mentally rehearsing being confident. This is using your imagination to practise, giving the brain strong positive images of how to behave in reality.

- Reviewing any situation either where you were confident or where you wished you had been more confident. Ask yourself what you did or what you could have done? Learn from the experience.

- Celebrating your successes.

- Breaking down any task into smaller, more achievable and less daunting ones.

GAINING EXPERIENCE

There are many ways to gain any experience you need. If it is not possible, for whatever reason, to go on a course or to do any formal retraining for what you want, you could always gain experience, and learn new skills at the same time, by:

- doing voluntary work – in the evenings or at weekends if you are in a Monday–Friday 9–5 job

- taking a part-time job

- shadowing people doing what you are interested in.

EXPLORING OPPORTUNITIES

> Whatever change you want in your life, it is important to explore all the opportunities open to you, even the ones you have not thought of yet!

Creating more choice

Thinking creatively (see more on this in Chapter 9) may reveal more choices than you had originally thought. Just let your mind wander by thinking 'What if nothing was stopping me? What would I do then?'

For instance, Josh was bored in his present job but did not really want to change as it had potential for him in the future. He wanted to take time out to travel but did not want to lose the security of his job. He read an article about working abroad as a volunteer and decided to ask his employer if he could take a sabbatical. This gave him exactly what he wanted.

Taking time out
Some employers may look on sabbaticals as a good career move, particularly if you use the time to improve your skills, such as learning a new language or gaining useful experience, maybe by working for a charity or working for an overseas organisation. Taking time out to do something different will certainly change your perspective on your current life.

Giving permission for minds to roam
What else could you do that at first may not seem possible? Ask friends and family for their ideas too, no matter how daft they might believe them to be. Tell them that all ideas are welcome. You may be surprised at how many 'solutions' suddenly exist once people feel free to express themselves, without constraint or fear of ridicule. Once you have lots of ideas, then you can begin to explore their reality.

Networking
The more people you know, the more likely it is that opportunities will open up to you. By building up a network of contacts, you are:

- giving yourself the chance to obtain information which may eventually lead to a job opportunity, if that is what you want

- gaining informal access to the hidden job market – to jobs that may not even exist yet or which have not yet been or may never be advertised

- raising your profile

- gaining a support group by meeting people with similar aims and needs

- meeting people you know or do not know, talking to them, learning from them and gaining information and new contacts.

Creating your network
Start by deciding who your contacts are. Make a list of anyone you meet – anyone at all – as you go about your daily work and play. They may be people you know well such as friends, family and neighbours or people you know less well such as colleagues, teachers, lecturers,

friends of friends, acquaintances, and so on. Now decide how each of them can help you (and if possible, how you can help them). Mothers with children at school are instinctive networkers. They meet at the school gate and learn where the babysitting circles are and who to contact in an emergency for school runs.

To widen the network even further, ask your friends, family, colleagues, friends of friends, acquaintances, and so on for the names of people they know who could help you and add them to your list.

Making contact
The next stage is to choose who you are going to approach first and to set up a meeting (either informally or formally, depending on who it is). It is important that you are clear at the beginning about what you want from the meeting. Remember that you may only have a short time to get your message across. Draw up a list of questions you might ask. They may include some of the following:

● Suggestions about career direction.

● Information about a particular organisation – people, aims, objectives, types of work, current projects.

● Developments within the career area or organisation.

● Ideas or suggestions about skills or attributes you may need to work on.

● Comments on your CV if relevant or appropriate.

● Names of anyone else who could help you.

Remember to add any new names to your ever-growing list of contacts. Consider how you might help people in return, either now or in the future.

Enjoying the process
Remember that any contact is a useful source of information and advice and may get you a step nearer to what you want. It is also possible that you may have an interesting and fun time in the process by meeting and talking with people. You will almost certainly learn something new from the experience too.

Getting hold of information
Libraries, colleges, career service companies, Business Links and TECs/LECs are all good sources of advice and information. Find out

where your local ones are by looking in the telephone directory and use them to your advantage.

CASE STUDIES

Jon seizes his opportunities

Jon was a programme researcher with one of the major television companies. He wanted to work in the TV and film industry but was not totally satisfied with what he was doing. He wanted to be more involved on the production side. He took every opportunity he was given to go on technical training courses. He also developed his knowledge by continually asking questions of other people. He eventually learnt enough to set up his own video production business.

Ailsa gains useful experience

Ailsa was bored with being at home. Both daughters were now at school and she had time on her hands. She had done retail work years ago before the children were born, but was finding it hard to persuade companies to give her a permanent retail post. A large department store was asking for temporary staff for the Christmas period and so she decided to apply. At the end of her contract they asked her to stay on permanently.

Bob and Chris combine their skills

Bob and Chris worked for a large engineering company. Neither was progressing within the company as he felt he should. They wondered if they could set up their own business. They did an inventory of their skills and attributes and realised they complemented each other, one having sales and marketing skills and the other financial expertise. Their aim was to recruit people for the technical side of the business. They researched the market and built up a network of contacts before handing in their notice. They are both now owners of a thriving business.

CHECKLIST

1. Can you identify what skills employers are currently looking for? Check out the advertisements and business sections in newspapers.

2. Keep learning and retraining, adding transferable and marketable skills to your repertoire.

3. How well can you answer the questions most often asked by interviewers?

4. How effective is your CV? Do you know who could help you with it?

5. What skills do you have already? Is the list getting longer?

6. Which new skills do you most need now? How can you learn them?

7. Would going back to education help? What courses does your local college offer for adults? Are there any correspondence courses suitable for your needs?

8. If you are looking for work, what can you do now to gain new skills and experience?

9. What opportunities are open to you now?

5

Managing Your Mind

By learning how to manage your thoughts you can change your behaviour and vice-versa. This means you can also change your experience of situations and people and influence the reactions you get from others. Once you are able to do this, you can then create your own future, by managing your mind in the way that works best for you.

UNDERSTANDING DIFFERENT EXPERIENCES

When walking on a beach in the height of summer, what do you see, hear and feel? Some people see only the crowds, children playing, adults sunbathing; others see the spaces between the people, the golden sand leading down to the sea; some of us will hear the noise of people talking, shouting and screaming; others will focus only on the sounds and smells of the sea; some will feel tension, others excitement. The difference is not in the beach scene but in each and every one of us. It all depends on who we are and how we experience our world.

The way we choose to respond to the world impacts on our behaviour, our thoughts and our future. It dictates whether we expect the worst or the best to happen; whether we enjoy our job or not. It is the reason why there are optimists and pessimists; why there are those who whinge about their life and those who decide to do something about it. Which kind of person are you and which kind do you want to be from now on? The choice is yours. Do you want to be someone who sees only the hole in the middle of the doughnut, or the person who looks at the doughnut itself?

Changing meanings

Depending on how you view a situation, you will feel differently about it and alter your behaviour accordingly. For example, if you have a long car or train journey to get to work and you see that as boring and a waste of time, you will almost certainly not enjoy it. However, if you see it as an opportunity, for example, to:

● listen to music

59

● catch up on reading (only on the train, not while driving the car!)

● maybe learn something new from audio tapes, providing it does not distract you from your driving

then you will probably enjoy the trip.

The important thing to remember is that we all have a **choice** about the meanings we give to situations.

From boring to stimulating

Think now of a situation about which you are unhappy. Perhaps if you gave a different meaning to it, you might be happier. For instance, can you make a boring task an exciting one, just by adding a little imagination? Maybe set yourself targets, in terms of speed or accuracy, to beat as you do it. Or while your unconscious mind concentrates on the task in hand, use your conscious mind to make those plans you never seem to have time for. From then on, you may regard boring tasks as opportunities for 'time out'.

Challenging yourself

We all know people we sometimes find annoying. However, the next time you find yourself thinking of someone in this way, do this instead:

● Take on the challenge of looking at them differently this time, as if seeing them for the first time.

● Look at them objectively, maybe from someone else's point of view if that is helpful.

● Concentrate on their good points, not their bad (we all have good points, some people's are just well hidden).

● Think of at least ten good things about them.

How does this change things for you?

Most people moan from time to time about problems and things they feel they cannot change. When you find yourself doing that, consider instead what it would take to move things forward or in a different direction. Think about how to put a different meaning on things. Focus on the present or the future not the past. Notice how that changes your perspective. People create more choices by looking at things from a different point of view. By doing this, you may be surprised at how much better your life suddenly becomes.

BEING RESPONSIBLE FOR YOUR OWN ACTIONS

Having the power to choose

We all have at least two choices. We can choose to be happy or sad, hardworking or lazy, optimistic or pessimistic, and so on. Once you realise this, it increases your confidence because it means you are in control and do not have to leave things to fate, to chance. Having choices means you have greater freedom to act. It is your choice how you respond. No one else's. We are all 'response-able' – we have the ability to respond as we wish to any situation.

Responding at will

This is why some people see beginnings and others see endings in some situations (see the case study at the end of this chapter). They are responding differently. Can you think of any events in your working life where you had the ability to respond in at least two different ways? For example:

- being passed over for promotion/accepting promotion

- getting a job/not getting a job

- being made redundant

- changing responsibilities

- being headhunted.

How does it change the situation when you have two responses available? Someone who has been passed over for promotion may think 'Oh well, why bother with anything any more? I'll never get anywhere in this place. My face obviously doesn't fit...' or 'Oh well, better luck next time. Perhaps if I work harder and smarter, I can show them how I deserve to be promoted.' Two separate responses, two separate behaviours.

Even something that is generally seen as a positive situation by most people opens itself up to a minimum of two responses and consequently differences in behaviour. Accepting an unexpected promotion can be seen in terms of 'I'll do my best to show I deserve this' or 'I wonder why they chose me? I'm not sure I can do the job!'. One response is very positive and full of confidence, the other shows uncertainty and lack of self-esteem. Each response will be reflected in the subsequent behaviour. Each response is a choice that we all have. Make sure yours is the one that works best for you.

FINDING OUT HOW TO BE LUCKY

Why do some people seem to have all the luck while others proclaim 'I'm never lucky'? Is it just luck? Or is there more to it? Many people believe that success is often down to luck. This may be true in some cases, but if anyone relies entirely upon luck for their success, then he or she is likely to be disappointed. It is far better and more certain to make your own luck. There are many ways to do this.

Allowing good luck in

Celebrity cook Madhur Jaffrey was once quoted as saying 'I'm always on the lookout for good luck. My door is usually open. I let the light in'. The key is in the words 'my door is usually open' – she is opening herself up to being lucky. This is something we can all learn to do.

You must first answer honestly the following four questions:

1. Are you willing to open yourself up to luck – to trust the universe to give you the opportunities you want?

2. Do you know what you want? Exactly what luck do you need?

3. Are you prepared for your good luck when it comes? (Remember King Midas and his touch of gold?)

4. Do you feel you deserve it?

If you answered 'yes' to all of the above then you are on the road to being lucky. If you answered 'no', then maybe it would be helpful to explore your reasons for doing so.

Opening up to luck
What stops you opening your mind to the possibility of good luck? What would it be like if you did? You may want to start by experimenting with your language (see 'Putting it all into practice' below) and noticing how your luck changes. You can also make some appropriate affirmations (see Chapter 3), such as:

- 'I am a lucky person.'

- 'I open myself up to all the good opportunities the universe has for me.'

What other affirmations might work for you?

Knowing what you want
Now you know what you want in life, it should be easy to know exactly

what form your good luck could take. What would make things even better for you? Specifically?

Preparing for good luck
What you get is precisely what you expect and believe you will get. It is therefore important, as stated earlier, to be prepared for having what you want. Imagine yourself in the future having achieved your goal. Is it really what you wanted? Or do you want to make some amendments to your plans and dreams? Now is the time to do it. Then you can be sure you are ready for your good luck when it comes.

Deserving it
Feeling you do not deserve any good luck, or that you are unworthy of it, is often a barrier to having it. This belief often means that you will not allow yourself to have good luck. It sends negative messages to your unconscious mind and, some believe, out to the universe. You will not then be attracting good luck. Does not everyone deserve to have some lucky breaks in their lives? Believe you deserve good luck and that you will succeed. There is more on the power of beliefs in the next chapter.

Attracting luck to you
Someone who is feeling lucky will look and be different to someone who has the belief that they are never lucky. Because mind and body are related, it is possible to give out different vibrations based on how you feel. If you do not believe this, try Activity 8. It is often said that you get what you focus on. So it is important to make sure you focus on what you want and thereby draw it to you. Think big. Think lucky.

Visualising
Picture what you want in terms of luck. Picture receiving it. As before in visualisation exercises, make sure you are looking through your own eyes, not seeing yourself from a distance. It makes it more real. Make the images in your mind as clear, as bright and as large as you can. Experiment with changing the size, colour and brightness of your mind pictures and notice how your feelings change too.

Feeding the mind
Whatever we believe determines the results we achieve. Why not believe in having the best luck? Feed your mind with positive thoughts and affirmations, such as those above. Your unconscious mind works continuously whether you are awake or asleep. Remember you have the

---

Activity 8 – Changing vibrations

● As an experiment, when you get out of bed tomorrow, decide you got out on the right side and believe the saying that 'when you smile, the whole world smiles with you'. When you go into work or into town shopping, you find it is easy to smile at people and have only good thoughts about them. Notice your experiences and the reactions of others to you.

● Now, on another day (but not for long!), decide to get out of bed the wrong side and believe the whole world is against you. Notice what happens when you meet other people.

How different were the two experiences? What you believe and how you behave affects the type of people you draw towards you and how they react to you.

---

power to feed your mind with whatever thoughts you choose. So is it not a good idea to make them thoughts that work for your highest good?

GAINING CONFIDENCE

A lack of confidence is often the biggest barrier to achieving what you want. Ways of overcoming this have already been mentioned (Chapters 3 and 4).

Anchoring your resources

Another way of accessing resources such as confidence is called **anchoring**. Remember how certain things can recall memories and emotions? Couples just have to hear 'their tune' to remember particularly good times. If your mother or father say your name in a certain way, you can be like a child again, knowing you are in trouble. Particular smells and tastes are very effective in triggering memories of previous experiences. A little whiff of country or sea air can bring back a flood of memories, feelings and experiences.

If certain senses can trigger memories, why not:

● recall times when you were resourceful

● use an appropriate trigger to 'anchor' the resource (to reconnect you to positive feelings)

● activate the anchor to access the resource any time you want.

Activity 9 takes you through the process of anchoring resources. You do not have to limit yourself to anchoring only confidence. By using different anchors you can have access to any number of different resources. Experiment anchoring positive resources. Notice what happens when you can control your own mind and behaviour.

PUTTING IT ALL INTO PRACTICE

Now is the time to put all of the above into practice. For example:

● Only admit thoughts into your mind which you choose and which contribute towards what you want.

● Challenge yourself to use positive language both in your thoughts and in your conversation for a week and notice what difference it makes to you. Each time you catch yourself saying things like 'Knowing my luck... I will never be able to...I always get it wrong... I never get it right', change immediately to something like 'I might get it right this time' or 'I can do it'. Keep doing this until you naturally state things more positively.

● Begin to expect the best, not the worst. Does this make a difference to your frame of mind? And to those around you?

● Change your physiology: stand more upright, walk more confidently. Look up, not down. Smile more.

● Look for the positive not the negative in things.

● Think of any change in your life as an opportunity rather than a threat and give yourself the best chance to have the working life you enjoy. Open yourself up to opportunities and good luck.

By practising changing your thoughts and your behaviour, you will learn to harness the power of your mind to create the working life you want. You will be in control.

CASE STUDIES

Rose makes her own luck

Rose wanted desperately to be a doctor, but thought she had left it too late at the age of 30. After being rejected by several medical schools, she was ready to give up. Then she met a couple of women in their 50s who

Activity 9 – Anchoring your resources

Anchoring confidence

1. Make sure you will be undisturbed for about 15 minutes or so. First choose your anchor or anchors. You should choose something that is easy to access and is meaningful. For instance, for confidence, some people use a closed fist or a gentle tap on the thigh. Think about where you will want to use this anchor and what would be most appropriate. Some people add in additional anchors such as an inner voice saying 'Go for it!' or something else appropriate, or something visual to trigger the anchor, such as seeing an audience in their mind's eye or a specific situation where they need to feel confident.

2. Now think of times when you were confident. Some people find it easier to close their eyes at this point. What do you know you do well and are confident about? From all the times you remember, recall the specific time when you were feeling at your most confident. Go back into the experience as if it were happening now. Look through your own eyes in your mind. What are you seeing, feeling, hearing? Allow yourself to be in the experience for a while until the feeling of confidence becomes strong. When you feel that you are coming to the peak of your confidence (you could not possibly feel any more confident), use the trigger(s) you have chosen (called 'firing the anchor') to reconnect your feelings and experiences.

3. Now open your eyes (if they were closed), move about and look around you to come out of the experience and back fully to the present.

4. Repeat the process (steps 2 and 3) until the anchor(s) and the feelings are really connected. People often do this about three to five times.

5. Test the anchor by making the gesture, saying or hearing the words and seeing the image, without thinking of the experience first. If you were fully in the experience when you fired the anchor before, you will now re-experience the feeling of confidence.

This works best if you have an experience to recall. However, if you really cannot think of any time when you were confident, think of a person you know who is confident. Imagine how that person would act in the situation in which you want to be confident. Make sure your physiology mirrors theirs and slowly imagine yourself becoming a confident person. What would you want to see, hear and feel? Imagine doing this as if it were the present. Then fire the anchors as above.

told her she was still a baby and had her whole life and every opportunity ahead of her.

She managed to persuade the next medical school to give her a chance and started a course as a single mum with a three-year-old in a strange new town. She now has only 18 months to go before qualifying and is living and loving her dream.

Nick changes his attitude

Nick had been self-employed for a couple of years but suddenly orders stopped coming in. He started to get depressed about it. Unsurprisingly it affected the way he was perceived by others. With drooping shoulders and a long face, he would tell people that things were not going too well. He was jealous of those who were successful. A friend told him that he was not giving a good impression and that people did not want to be with him because he appeared so negative.

He started acting as if things were going well. He stood more upright and smiled at people, saying with a firm voice that business was improving. He actually felt more confident. This gave him more energy and he began to have ideas about how to improve his business. Some of them worked.

Mike and Joe hold differing views

Mike and Joe, old school friends, bumped into each other after many years of not being in contact. They discovered that their lives had great similarities. They had both been made redundant in the last six months. They were the same age, had been doing similar jobs for roughly the same number of years. There was, however, one big difference – their attitudes to life. Mike was convinced he would never work again and was complaining about his situation, saying it was not his fault and how awful it all was. Joe was positively radiant, saying that now he had the chance and the money to do what he had always wanted. He was going to travel the world for a while and was sure he could convince an employer to take him on when he returned. Two men in a similar situation with two totally different perspectives on it.

CHECKLIST

1. Experiment with your thoughts and your behaviour.

2. Notice how you experience the world. Become aware of how others view it differently.

3. How many choices can you generate by putting different meanings to different situations?

4. What events in your working life could you have responded differently to?

5. How much good luck are you willing to allow into your life?

6. What resources would you like to anchor and have access to whenever you want?

7. How many of the points under 'Putting it all into practice' will you practise tomorrow?

8. Are you using the power of your mind to realise your full potential?

6

Believing in Yourself

Whatever we believe determines the results we achieve.

IDENTIFYING YOUR BELIEFS

What we believe has enormous effect on our lives. For instance, if we do not believe that fire is hot, that there are sharks in some seas, that we cannot fly of our own accord, and so on, we could end up hurt a lot of the time. Beliefs are important to us.

How we get our beliefs

We acquire our beliefs through our own and other people's experience. We test them out first of all to see if they are true. If the evidence supports the belief, we tend to believe it. See below for examples of supporting evidence. Beliefs are also self-perpetuating. For instance, if you believe you are weak, you probably are. If you believe you are going to be a success, the chances are you will be. Remember that the mind is very powerful and reacts to the messages it is given. This is why placebos sometimes work instead of the real thing.

Limiting or empowering?

You can change direction at any time in your life. The only thing that prevents you is your belief in your limitations. Beliefs can be useful or not useful. For instance, a belief in your potential for success is a useful one if you are to get the job you want or turn a hobby into a money-making enterprise. A belief that you will 'never get anywhere' might just limit that potential! Activity 10 gives you the opportunity to examine the beliefs you currently hold and decide which ones limit you and which ones empower you.

How many of your beliefs in what is possible determined what has happened in your life? Have they held you back or pushed you forward?

Activity 10 – Beliefs you hold

1. On a sheet of paper, complete the following sentences, writing at least three things for each one. If you really cannot think of anything, look at the examples given to give you some ideas. However, it is better to let your mind be creative and come up with whatever it wants to, without being guided by the examples. Cover them up if necessary.

I'm the sort of person who...
(*eg* never achieves anything; always finishes a job; has great ideas; just is not creative; doesn't deserve to succeed; will go far.)

I am...
(*eg* a bad speller; hopeless with figures; great with children; good at my job; successful in all I do.)

Life is...
(*eg* a ball, like a roller coaster, a constant battle, a game, a bowl of cherries.)

2. What beliefs do you hold about:

Money...
(*eg* it makes the world go round; it only comes to those who ask; it doesn't grow on trees.)

Work...
(*eg* you have to work hard to get anywhere; everyone has to work; work should be fun.)

Success...
(*eg* success comes to those who work for it; success breeds success; anyone can be successful if they want to.)

Time...
(*eg* there's never enough time; time waits for no man; you can always make time if you want.)

3. Put a cross against those beliefs that limit you in some way and a tick against those that you find empowering and useful to hold. You might wish to change the limiting ones. What would be more useful to believe? Experiment writing down more useful beliefs. How does it feel?

SUPPORTING EVIDENCE

Believe it or not

Our childhood belief in the existence of Father Christmas was upheld by various facts:

- Our parents, figures of authority who always told the truth, told us he was real.

- We had to put out mince pies and sherry or something similar for him.

- We often saw him in the flesh in a Santa Claus grotto.

- He was depicted on Christmas cards.

- We wrote to him.

- He left us presents.

It is quite a long list of evidence to support the fact that he exists – who were we, little children, to disbelieve? Many of our beliefs exist because of what we learnt or experienced of the world at a much younger age. If you did believe in Father Christmas at one time, it is highly likely that you no longer believe in him now (sorry, he was never real!). You changed your belief, yet the evidence was very powerful and made for a powerful belief. So it is possible to change what you believe.

Making it real for you

The brain cannot distinguish between what is real and what is not. To take an example, imagine now that you are holding a lemon. It is big and very yellow. You take a sharp knife and slowly slice through it. As you do this, some of the juice spurts up and hits you on the face. You lick your lips and taste the bitterness of the fruit. Did you salivate at any time during that description? Now picture a blackboard just like you had at school. Someone is standing in front of it and has long fingernails. She scrapes them slowly down the board and you can hear the grating noise very clearly. Did you wince when you read that?

Both the above descriptions were simply that – descriptions. They were not real. You did not really taste lemon juice (is your saliva running again?) nor did you hear the fingernails scraping the blackboard (ooh, stop!). Your brain, however, could not tell the difference. Your body reacted as if you were experiencing reality.

Similarly, our memories can deceive us. How many people share an experience and yet, when they each relate what happened, it is as if they were all in different places at different times with different people?

Siblings often have completely different accounts of shared experiences. Since the brain cannot tell the difference between something imagined and something real, how do we know what reality is? If we do not know what reality really is, then it is possible to create our own. Acting as if something were true gives you the possibility of 'trying on' new beliefs. You can act as if you believe you are whatever you want to be.

IMAGINING OTHERWISE

Our beliefs change as we change and learn more of the world. However, some beliefs are so powerfully instilled in us that we may think they are immutable. Would it not be wonderful to be able to change any of your beliefs when you want to? Imagine what it would be like if you believed you were capable of anything rather than hardly anything at all. Imagine if you believed you were successful in all you did, not a failure in many things. Imagine if you believed your future was bright, not dim.

Changing limiting beliefs

So how can you change a limiting belief to a more empowering one? The first step is to question your current belief. Is it useful to you at this time? If you decide it is not, regardless of whether you think it possible to believe otherwise:

> **Choose what you would rather believe or what would be more useful to believe.**

For instance, if you believe that you would never be successful, you might decide that you now want to change that to the more useful belief that you can be successful whenever you want. However, just saying it or writing it does not always make it true. It may be necessary to do more to change limiting beliefs. Taking the same example, you may want to:

- Gather supporting evidence for your new belief. Look into your past and note all your successes (refer back to Chapter 1 – Celebrating your achievements).

- Look around you for evidence to support the belief. Are there other people who believe it of you, or who have a similar belief which works for them?

- Ask yourself what it would cost you to continue with the old belief. What effect does it have on your life?

● Imagine what effect the new belief will have on your life. Try it on for size. Visualise yourself in the future with this new belief. How different and how much better could your life be?

● State your new belief out loud regularly until you begin to feel the difference. Remember the power of affirmations?

Try these steps out with one of the limiting beliefs you identified from Activity 10. Notice how you feel once you start to adopt the new belief. Beliefs should not be confused with wishful thinking. We can all wish we were more confident or better at doing something. Actually believing it will generate more power and energy. The mind will then develop ways of making it come true for you.

There are many other techniques used for changing beliefs which are detailed in NLP books (see Further Reading at the end of the book).

HAVING FUN

What difference would it make to you if you overturned some of your limiting beliefs? Instead of the inner voice that says 'I can't' or 'I'm not the type of person who does...', why not change it to one that says 'but what if I could...?', 'but what if I were...?'. You do not have to accept the new belief right away or even at all, but it could be enjoyable just to play with it. Children have great fun imagining what it would be like if things were different. Why should they have all the fun?

Expecting the best

If up until now you never expected to:

● do well at anything

● enjoy the work you do

● earn a lot of money

● be successful

why not begin to believe you could change? Expect the best from now on. Remember that you get more of what you focus on. So why not start with smaller expectations? If you believed that you were someone who could never find your keys, expect to find them from now on. If you believed that there are never any parking spaces when you want them, expect to find one now.

Alter your beliefs about your expectations. Change your inner voice to one that expects the best for you from now on. You may occasionally have to be patient as we do not always get what we want in the timescale we envisaged. Sometimes the universe has other plans for us! However, you may be surprised at how often you will now get the results you want.

Once some of your smaller, maybe less important, expectations begin to be fulfilled, have fun playing with bigger ones. Expect to find what you are looking for, whether it is a job or the opportunity of a lifetime. It has been said that we never rise higher than our aspirations. So expect great things of yourself. And enjoy what happens.

REINFORCING EMPOWERING BELIEFS

'Vision without action just passes the time, action without vision is merely a dream, vision plus action can change the world.' Anon.

It is vital that, having identified your empowering beliefs, you take action to reinforce them. Otherwise you could be wasting your time. You can reinforce beliefs by gathering as much evidence as you can to support them, particularly if they are new to you. Add new and powerful references. References are the personal experiences you have and the information you gain from other sources to support your beliefs. Such information includes that gained from people agreeing with you or from role models – people with a similar belief about themselves and who are achieving results.

You will find that when you believe in something wholeheartedly, your unconscious mind will come up with ways to support that belief. It then becomes self-fulfilling.

Once you have learnt to change your limiting beliefs to empowering ones, you may find you have established a powerful belief in your own potential. Until you believe in yourself it is likely that no one else will believe in you. So what are you waiting for?

CASE STUDIES

Trish acquires new beliefs

Trish (see Chapter 1) wanted to start earning some money. She had always believed she did not have any skills, but the realisation that she and her friends were in fact multi-skilled gave her the stimulus she needed. She persuaded one of her friends to do an adult education class in paint finishes with her. It was only a week course, but during that time they shared their dream of setting up a painting and decorating business with the other students. One of these students believed in them and gave them their first commission.

Jez enforces the belief

Jez (see Chapter 2) began to achieve the results he wanted once he had taken some positive steps towards realising his goal. Giving himself a deadline to work towards, telling his friends of his plans and asking his father for help, all enforced his belief that he would leave London soon.

Mike and Joe's contrasting beliefs

Mike (see Chapter 5) believed he would never work again. His whole physiology and behaviour helped to reinforce the belief He was perceived by employers as low in self-esteem and confidence. Joe on the other hand believed he would get work whenever he wanted it. Which of them is the more employable?

CHECKLIST

1. How many limiting beliefs did you hold?

2. Have you examined your past for any beliefs which might have held you back?

3. Which ones are you willing to change to those that empower you instead?

4. What exactly would you like to believe is true?

5. Decide which beliefs you will have fun with.

6. What will you expect of yourself from now on?

7. To what extent are you willing to believe in yourself?

7

Clarifying Your Objectives

PICKING UP YOUR DREAM

Someone once said that we create our tomorrows by what we dream today. If that is true, it is important to make sure our dreams are very clear, so that our tomorrows are what we want them to be. Vaguely expressed wishes rarely translate into the reality we expect. It is useful to do the following if you want things to happen:

1. Be clear about what you want (Chapter 2).

2. Know the reasons for your goal – what motivates you (Chapter 2).

3. Have a written definite plan of action (Chapter 3).

4. Be determined and persistent (Chapter 8).

5. Notice what you are getting and be prepared to change if necessary (this chapter).

By carrying out these five steps, you are well on the way to committing to and picking up your dream. You will be clear about what needs to be done and in what order. You will have the motivation to carry it through.

PUTTING IDEAS INTO PRACTICE

It is one thing having a goal or dream and quite another achieving it. This is where the 'definite plan of action' comes in. Having done Activity 5, Chapter 3, you have already identified your all-important first step.

What happens next is just as crucial if you are to pick up your dream.

Planning ahead

It helps to plan the various steps to be taken. A very useful planning tool is something which is sometimes called 'critical path analysis'. This is where you plan out all the various elements of a goal – exactly what needs to be done and when. You start by writing down what your goal is and the date by when you want to have achieved it. Now work backwards from that date. What needs to be in place for your goal to happen?

It may help if you mentally rehearse what is to happen in the future. If you can imagine yourself having achieved your goal, you might be able to work out what had to happen for you to arrive at your chosen destination.

For instance, if your goal is to be in a new job within twelve months, you may need to do some or all of the following:

● Carry out some research into the market place.

● Attend interviews.

● Rewrite your CV.

● Apply to companies.

● Develop new skills.

Now it is a simple matter of working out when each of these steps needs to take place and in what order. It often happens that one thing needs to occur before another, such as rewriting your CV before attending interviews. Doing a critical path analysis allows you to see what actions are dependent on other ones. It also helps you see how realistic you are being in terms of time.

Chunking down

Some goals are too big to tackle all at once. It therefore helps to chunk or break them down into more manageable steps. For example, if your dream is to become self-employed, you might want to break this goal down into various elements, which might include the following:

● Doing the necessary research on tax and insurance for the self-employed.

● Researching your market.

● Being absolutely clear on what you have to offer.

● Working out your pricing structure.

● Doing a business plan.

● Calculating what capital, if any, you will need.

Each element then becomes a goal in itself, with its own plan of action and the ability to be subdivided into even smaller elements if necessary. It does not matter how small each step is. The important thing is to do whatever it takes to work towards your goal. How could you break down your goal? What specific parts does it have?

KEEPING THE DREAM ALIVE

Sometimes circumstances prevent you from having what you want exactly when you want. For example, it may be that you cannot have the finance you need for a new venture for a few months or so; you may need to develop some new skills before being able to change jobs; someone else has influenced you to go down a different career path first; or you may have to wait until the children start school before you can choose what you want to do. Another frequent occurrence is that you get caught up in the minutiae of everyday living and your dream gets thrust to one side, in danger of being forgotten. It is important therefore to find ways to keep your dream alive and of reminding yourself that you have a goal in mind.

Using all the senses
The brain works best when all the senses are involved. It is therefore a good idea to use as many of your senses as possible and as appropriate to keep your dream alive.

For instance:

● Give your goal substance by writing it down (touch, sight).

● Mention it to other people (sound).

● Say it out loud to yourself (sound).

● Put it somewhere visible as a reminder (sight).

● Make a 'treasure collage'. This is where you use photos, drawings, pictures and words (maybe cut from old magazines and catalogues) to represent your goals visually. It can be fun to do, uses the senses of touch and sight and can also clarify exactly what you want. Notice what results you begin to achieve.

● Take some action, however small, every day towards your goal. This could be in the form of writing out a detailed plan of action, doing an affirmation, doing some research, networking, and so on.

DRAWING ON YOUR RESOURCES

Even if you believe that you have all the resources you need, it can sometimes be difficult to know initially what resources you require. If you do not know what these are, how can you draw on them? One way to find out is to do Activity 11. It involves you relaxing and tapping your unconscious mind for the resources you need. It may only take ten minutes or so of your time and could be well worth it.

You may have discovered that you need a variety of resources, such as information, role models or guides. Some might be external and others internal.

External
Mentor
Mentoring is currently popular in organisations and in government programmes, such as those helping disaffected young people back into education or training. A mentor is not necessarily someone you know well, but someone you feel comfortable with and whom you can talk to about any problems or challenges. Their role is to support you, acting either as a role model or as someone to motivate you or help you in your development. A mentor can also be a constant in your life when all else is changing.

Look at your networking list and pick out one or two people whom you might wish to consider as mentors. Approach them and ask if they would be willing to commit to supporting you in this way. Most people are flattered to be asked to do this. You are asking them to commit to meeting with you or contacting you regularly to see how things are going and what help you might need. They do not have to provide the help personally but help you identify where you might get it from.

Buddy
Having a friend to support you whenever you need it can be vital. He or she could be someone to 'bounce ideas off' or someone who is able to motivate you (perhaps by bullying you in the nicest possible way) at crucial times. Which of your friends would be willing to fulfil this role? Could you reciprocate?

Network
The importance of networks was discussed in Chapter 4. Who in your network can help you pursue your dream? Are you networking to advantage? Do you network 'on purpose', towards your dream?

Activity 11 – Finding out what resources you need

1. Make sure you will not be disturbed by the phone or by anyone interrupting you. Take a few moments to relax, by sitting down somewhere comfortable and closing your eyes. Now take a few deep breaths, breathing in slowly, deeply and gently, releasing any tension on the outbreath.

2. Focus on your immediate goal. Imagine being in the future having achieved what you wanted. Picture the scene as if you are there now; the future is now your present. What do you feel, see and hear? Make it as vivid as possible by making the scene colourful and bright and focused. Intensify any sounds.

3. Then in the position of having achieved your goal, look back to the past (remember that if you can be in the present and imagine the future, you can easily reverse the process).

4. What resources did you need to get to where you are now? What or who helped you? If it was you and no one else who helped you, what internal resources did you call upon? For example, did you use confidence, enthusiasm, a belief? What specific resources did you need? Did you use an inner voice to keep you on track?

5. Once you have identified the resources which were useful to you, whether they were internal or external, tangible or intangible, bring yourself slowly back to the present. Become aware once more of your breathing and the sounds of the room. Open your eyes and look around you, knowing that you are once more fully present in the here and now.

6. Write down or record in some way the thoughts that came to you as a result of this exercise.

Family
Unless your family knows of your plans, it is hard to expect them to support you. Many people are surprised at how much help they receive from people once they have shared their dreams with them. You might even find you have a common dream and can work towards it together. Think about exactly what support you might need from your family. Is it:

- practical (*eg* doing more chores to enable you to have some more free time or helping you with writing your CV or planning your next move)

- emotional (*eg* just letting you know that whatever happens they are there for you and support you wholeheartedly)

- financial (*eg* does the whole family need to cut back on luxuries to free up money to enable you to pursue your dream?)

- something else?

Friends
Friends can be very useful as a resource. They might be able to offer specific practical help or act as sounding boards for your ideas. They are often very willing to help in whatever way they can. Maybe you could set up a self-help group, where a few friends could identify exactly how they could all help each other work towards their dreams.

Children
Young people can act as inspiration, motivators and even as information givers. They do not tend to see as many obstacles to dreams as adults do. They can also be useful contacts as they know other children and through them you could be introduced to an adult who may be a good resource.

Organisations
There are many organisations that can give you the information you might need to pursue your dream, depending on what it is. The *Yellow Pages* is a useful source of information. Other sources include:

- banks

- Business Link

- careers service companies

- colleges

● libraries.

Books and other materials
There are books, tapes, videos and websites on almost any subject you could think of. Some useful relevant books are listed in Further Reading. Libraries are great for generating ideas (just by reading book titles in the business and careers sections) and giving you the resources to start you off in the right direction. Why not explore your local one to find out exactly what it has to offer?

Internal
Beliefs
Beliefs are powerful, whether they are limiting or empowering. Which do you want yours to be? If you need to do more work on making your beliefs work more usefully for you, go back to Chapter 6.

Messages
Many people talk of having a voice in their heads, 'a little voice says...', 'then I say to myself...', 'I hear my mother's/father's voice in my head...', and so on. What many of us fail to realise is that we can change these voices to whatever we want. We can change the messages they give and the way they give them. After all, our head is our own and with some application we can change what goes into and comes out of it. So if you have a voice that says something you do not particularly find useful, in a tone of voice that demotivates you or worse, change it!

Have fun experimenting with voices, tones, pitches and words. What would be most useful to hear? Next time you have that inner voice saying something you do not want, immediately change it to something more useful and more motivating for you. In time you will only hear the things that will be of most benefit to you.

Guides
Some people ask a 'higher source' for an internal guide. This usually involves allowing your unconscious mind to reveal your guide or guides to you. There are specific meditations on this, such as the one given in Gill Edwards' book *Living Magically*.

If this does not work for you or if you do not wish to use this method, you could still use the same concept. All you have to do is think of people you admire or respect. Now imagine what help or advice they would give to someone like you. What would they say or do in a similar situation? These people do not have to be living or even real. There may be a fictional character that is the perfect role model or guide for you.

Why not use all the resources available to you?

What other resources not mentioned above could you identify that would help you achieve your goal?

BEING FLEXIBLE

Noticing what you are getting

If you are not getting the response or the result you want, do something different. The old adage 'if at first you don't succeed, try, try and try again' works much better if the words 'another way' are added to it. Scientists would not get very far if they kept doing the same old thing all the time with the same end result. It is because they are flexible in their thinking that they make the progress they do. They notice the results they get and change their methods or approach accordingly.

The important thing is to notice what results you are getting. There is a great difference between being committed to your dream and being flexible if you are not getting what you want. For instance, if you want to find a way past a brick wall, would it be useful continually to bang your head against it? It would surely be more useful to explore other ways of getting through (under, round, over) it.

Only on hold

Occasionally dreams are put on hold, for whatever reason. It may be that the timing is not quite right or the finances are not yet available, or some other perfectly good reason. In these cases, it can be helpful to believe that the dream is only on hold and is not lost. For instance, you may want to:

- move out of your present job

- go back to work

- change an interest into a money-earning activity

and yet there are good reasons for not being able to do so at the present time.

Flexibility in your thinking can help you in this case. Instead of thinking you must achieve this goal now, know that you will have it when the time is right for you. Work towards it in whatever way you can, even if you cannot actually have it now. For instance, is there research you can carry out in the meantime; can you acquire skills or resources while you are waiting; can you earn money now which will help you in the future?

Provided you have your 'definite plan of action' for what you want, you will be able not only to keep hold of your dream but to continue to work towards it. Again, it is useful in this case to put your goal in writing and have it somewhere you can see it regularly so that you are constantly reminded of it and encouraged by it.

CASE STUDIES

Jeff is only postponing his dream, not cancelling

Jeff wanted to be an artist. He had the talent, having already at a young age had some of his work exhibited in galleries. His parents, however, were worried that it was not a secure means of earning a living. They persuaded him to do academic A-levels. Jeff did a languages degree and became an interpreter, travelling and working overseas for an international organisation. He was so busy that he rarely had the time to paint even as a hobby.

However, he was occasionally troubled by the fact that he had not pursued his dream of being a painter. One day a friend saw some of Jeff's work and asked him when he was going to take up painting seriously. Jeff realised then that he had not lost his dream, only postponed it. He still had the talent. All it required was some planning to find the time to paint and the belief that he was still good. Who knows, eventually he might even be able to make it his full-time occupation if that is what he wants.

Marie clarifies her goal

Marie felt frustrated being stuck at home with young children. She wanted a career that would enable her to work from home, but could not think of what to do. A friend suggested she write down all the things she knew for certain she wanted, such as working from home, ability to take holidays and other time off when she wanted, working with people, work that enabled her to learn new things, and so on. She did this and also added her own skills, abilities and the resources available to her (a spare room which could be used as an office, for instance). Some time later she was treated to a massage for her birthday and through talking to her aromatherapist, the idea came to her that she could explore the possibility of training in some area of beauty therapy. This would give her all the things she had written down!

Paul uses all available resources

Paul was unhappy in his job as an insurance salesman. He did not know what else he wanted to do, except that it had to be something completely different. He began asking all his friends about their jobs, what they liked about them and what they did not. Three of his friends were teachers. The more he found out about teaching, the more he was sure that this was what he wanted to do. His friends arranged for him to have some work experience in their schools so he could experience primary and secondary teaching. He decided primary teaching was for him and that he could use the money he had earned from his insurance job to see him through the teacher training.

CHECKLIST

1. How clear are you about your objectives? Are they written down?

2. Have you tried using a critical path analysis to plan in what order to do things?

3. How many ways can you think of to keep your dream alive?

4. Exactly what resources do you need to help you pursue your objective?

5. How many of them are external, how many internal?

6. Remember to notice what results you are getting. Do you need to change any of your plans in any way?

8

Identifying Obstacles

Many of us have goals but not all of us achieve them. Why? It's usually because we feel something or someone stops us. You have by now stated your goal and made it compelling. In this chapter we look at any obstacles in your way and how to overcome them.

BEING REALISTIC

Identifying the blocks to success

Often when someone has a dream or a goal, or wants to change his or her life in some way, a little voice inside says 'yes, but...'. If you do not have this inner voice, the chances are someone else will say 'yes, but...' instead! Think now of any of your own plans that you are not carrying forward for some reason. List yours or other people's objections to them. Your list may include:

- Finance – how will you get it if you need it to start up your own business, to pay for training, or to support you and your family while you research your next move?

- Children – who will look after them?

- Partner and friends – will you have time to give to relationships?

- The home – how will you do all the chores and everything else that needs doing if you are involved in your career?

- Age – you are too old, or too young.

- Lack of training and skills – you have not got what it takes.

- Lack of opportunity – there are no jobs available for what you want to do.

GIVING YOURSELF MORE CHOICES

The list above is long enough. Was yours as long or even longer? We are all used to looking for obstacles. Instead why not focus more often on how we could make things work? Concentrate on the 'how I could' and not the 'why I can't'? Why not train yourself to look for the possibles and not the impossibles in a situation?

Looking for possibilities is not just about positive thinking, although this does of course help. It is also about making more choices for yourself. If you can train your mind to think of ways to overcome obstacles, the chances are you will find the way that makes the difference, the one that works. If instead you only think of the obstacle and how it is blocking you, you may find your mind is set on coming up with even more obstacles for you to overcome. The outcome of this is likely to be inaction through overload of problems.

What do you do if you are out walking and you encounter something blocking your path? Or if you are in a car and you come across a fallen tree in the road? Do you:

● stay exactly where you are and worry about the consequences of missed appointments? Or do you

● take some form of action such as removing the obstacle, going round it, or turning back and taking a different route altogether?

Which of the two is more useful to do? Which one gives you more choices?

The techniques detailed in the next chapter will encourage your creative juices to flow, thereby generating possible ways round your problem, whatever it is.

TAKING A CHANCE

People often resist doing something new or different for one or more of the following reasons:

● Fear – of the unknown (the *status quo* is familiar).

● Fear – of a loss of control (the *status quo* is safe).
● Fear – of uncertainty (it may not work, so why try?).

● Fear – of more effort needed (maintaining the *status quo* may be easier and more comfortable).

● Fear – of failure (people might find you out – your dreams are safe, reality might be different).

● Fear – of insecurity (taking a risk is risky!).

Fear is one of the biggest obstacles stopping people doing what they want and taking control of their own career. Does any of this sound familiar to you?

Either you do something or you have all the excuses why not. Naomi was convinced she would climb the Gloucester tree (65 metres high), south of Perth in Australia. She had read about it many months beforehand and wanted to do it, even though she knew it would be a huge challenge for her. When she got there and started on the bottom rung, she was feeling OK and thought she could still do it. Only a few rungs further up, she felt the flutterings of fear and apprehension and decided that:

- the steel rungs on the ladder were making her fingers cold which meant that she might lose her grip higher up

- she was not wearing the right shoes and might slip

- she might not be able to get down if she became even more scared at the top

- it was getting dark and she might not be able to see if she went any higher

- the wind was getting up and the ladder might start to shake.

She got no further.

All Naomi's excuses might have been valid. She may have known herself well enough to realise she was at the edge of her limitations. However, once she allowed fear to take hold of her, she came up with dozens of excuses to back out. She questioned none of them. They were all based on what might go wrong. Her fear did not allow her to think about what made her want to be there in the first place – the sense of achievement, the view from the top, the exhilaration of climbing the famous tree. Fear effectively paralysed her. You could say, of course, that at least she started the climb. The point is that she did not give herself enough of a chance to complete it, but gave up at almost the first hurdle (or rung).

Have you ever done this? How many excuses do you have for not going for that new job or promotion, not trying that new venture, not taking a calculated risk?

Fears can stop us, like Naomi's did, literally in our tracks. Someone once said that 'courage is not the absence of fear but the ability to carry on with dignity in spite of it.' So it is OK to feel afraid, but do not let it control you. Ask yourself 'what is the worst thing that can happen?'

Once you have acknowledged that, it somehow seems easier to confront your fear.

Using fear to advantage

Fears can be useful indicators for what might lie ahead. They may help you decide your next step or ensure you have contingency plans in place. Once you have identified exactly what your own fears are, the important thing is to examine them closely. For instance, if you are afraid to apply for a particular job, ask yourself first of all why you are afraid. Exactly what is holding you back? Then ask yourself if your fear is justified. If it is, is there any way you or someone else can allay it? Or is your fear letting you know that perhaps you are not ready for a new job yet, but may need to do some preparation first? Fear of going in one direction can propel you to explore other avenues.

Fear can also be useful, in that it supplies the adrenalin we need to get through a daunting task. Actors and presenters often say they are really scared before every performance. The adrenalin produced by fear and apprehension helps our reactions and also gives us the means to make sure we prepare enough in advance. If we did not have the fear, we might not be prepared for what happens.

Susan Jeffers in her book *Feel the Fear and Do It Anyway* advises us to turn our fears into confidence and action. Maybe we also need to confront them to find out how real they are and what they are telling us before doing something about them.

Imagining success

One way around your fears could be to imagine what it would be like if nothing was holding you back. For instance, it may be that:

- the future is unknown

- you are not sure that you will succeed

- you do not know where you will get the money from

- you are unclear about what effort you need to put in

- you have no idea whether you will have an easy or a hard ride towards your goal.

These are all unknowns possibly keeping you from your goals. What would happen if the future was exactly how you wanted it to be? How different would it be if you knew for certain that you would succeed, that you would find ways of raising money if you needed it, that you were able and willing to put in the amount of effort required and that you would have an easy ride?

Take a quiet moment or two to imagine yourself in the future, with all the above in place and you having succeeded at whatever it is you want. You have taken control of your own career and are exactly where you want to be. Remember previous exercises where you were looking through your own eyes, hearing any sounds and feeling as if the future was really the present. What exactly do you see, hear and feel?

Back in the present, having had a taste of the future and with that vision in front of you and your strength of purpose behind you, how does your future look now? Are you able to express your goals more clearly? Do you feel you might hit the mark? And are your fears any smaller or less significant now? Having mentally rehearsed the future, you have already given your unconscious the appropriate messages you want it to act upon and given yourself more of a chance of success. Why not also write down how you imagined the future? In this way you give your imagination some concrete substance.

Letting go

The future need not contain any limitation because it does not yet exist so therefore you can create whatever you like. The only limitations are those you place on yourself. You may want to try Activity 12 which allows you literally to get rid of all that is holding you back and experience what it is like to be free of all limitations.

LEARNING FROM EXPERIENCE

Experience is how we learn. That is why employers value it so much. It is an indication of what we have learnt and are capable of doing to date. Unfortunately, experiences are not always good. However, we can always learn something even from bad experiences. We might not always recognise the learning immediately and we may not even want to, but nevertheless the learning is there, whether it is about ourselves or about other things.

Looking at things from a different angle

Bad experiences can often stop us from moving forward. You may be rejected for a job or a new venture and decide not to try again. It is often useful with bad experiences to use a technique called 'reframing', where you learn to put a different slant on things, to look at things with a new perspective. It enables you to see if there is a more positive way of viewing the situation.

Activity 12 – Getting rid of the hold-ups

1. Write down on pieces of paper everything that is holding you back. One limitation per piece of paper.

2. Once you have quite a pile, take each one in turn, look at it and then screw it up and put it in a bin.

3. Now take a deep breath in and really let go of all those limitations with the outbreath. If you had lots of limitations, you may need to take another couple of deep breaths in and out, letting more go with each breath, until they are all quite gone and definitely in that bin.

4. How does it feel being free of all limitations? Now is a good time to let your imagination have free rein. Explore all the possibilities now available to you. What chances do you want to take? What risks might be acceptable?

5. You may wish to record any thoughts on new pieces of paper and keep them somewhere handy.

Remember: you can have your limitations back any time you want. Or you can leave them in the rubbish bin. The choice, as ever, is yours.

For instance, if you failed to persuade your boss to allow you to take on more responsibility, a reframe might be something like 'well, without extra responsibility, you will have more time to concentrate on x, y or z' or 'maybe it is time to take your career in a different direction'.

The belief that 'there is no failure, only feedback' is a good example of a reframe. Think about how wonderful it would have been for some of us if we had known this in our school days. How much more might we all have achieved had we known that we could not fail, only learn? That so-called failures were simply experiences teaching us something? Scientists know this well. They even make new discoveries when experiments go wrong. New recipes are created when cooks mix the 'wrong' ingredients or make mistakes in measuring. What mistakes, bad experiences or failures are there in your recent past? Think about how you could reframe them and learn from them.

No experience is wasted.

MOVING ON

If you are unhappy about actions you have taken in the past, remember that the past is over and the future is yet to come. If you believe you learn from mistakes, then by making them, you will be learning. Learn to celebrate your mistakes instead of crying over them. Why not have fun and make mistakes every day?

When teaching people to juggle, it helps to have them cheer out loud every time they drop a ball. In this way they are learning that each thud of the ball is yet another way they have learnt not to juggle. They are therefore one step closer to juggling. How can you relate this to your goal?

Having identified any obstacles in your way, acknowledged any fears holding you back and experienced letting go of your limitations, you have mentally rehearsed the future you want. Now is the time to move on to the next chapter where you will engage your whole being to start the process of creative thinking. This will help you move closer to the future you have already envisaged.

'The vision to see, the faith to believe, and the will to do will take you anywhere you want to go.' Anon.

CASE STUDIES

Val overcomes obstacles

When Val was made redundant from her secretarial job, she was two months pregnant with her third child. She had always intended to go back to work after having her baby. Not being entitled to any redundancy pay, she temped up to the day before the baby was due, making good contacts for the future. She decided to set up her own secretarial service company, taking in typing. However, she had no money to buy her own equipment. Val said she had 'always believed there's a solution to everything' and found a friend who let her hire a computer until she could afford to buy it. She now employs 26 home-working mothers and made a profit in 1997 of £50,000.

Mark takes a risk

Mark had always wanted to be an actor. However, due to parental pressure, he went into teaching. He started a drama class and took the occasional role in school performances. At the age of 27, he decided he had had enough of teaching, left his steady job and signed on as an actor. He has already had some bit parts in various television productions and feels confident that his big chance will come soon: 'If you want to do something and feel you can achieve it, you can'.

CHECKLIST

1. How many blocks to success have you identified?

2. What do you do when you encounter an obstacle?

3. What is holding you back from being in control of your career now?

4. Start confronting your fears. Do something this week that you have been afraid to do.

5. How many mistakes are you going to have fun making today?

6. Have you taken time to experience your future?

7. How many limitations have you let go? How does it feel?

8. What reframes can you put on your so-called mistakes or failures?

9

Generating Creative Thinking

FOCUSING ON THE CRUX OF THE MATTER

Identifying the problem

Only once you have identified exactly what the problem is can you begin to solve it. Take your list of objections to your goal from the last chapter. Is there any particular one that is a major stumbling block to your goal? Or are they all equal? Be absolutely clear about what is stopping you moving forward or you may find that once you have solved one problem, you come up with another.

It can be useful at this point to look at each obstacle in turn, if there are more than one, and to become very specific about what it is that is blocking you. For instance, let us take some of the obstacles listed in the previous chapter:

- If lack of money is your problem and you are saying to yourself something along the lines of 'I don't have any money to start my own business' or 'I can't get another job because it won't pay as well as this one', have you asked yourself questions, such as 'How much money do I need to start my own business? How much money do I need to live on? Specifically?'

- If you have children and want to go back to work, what exactly is the problem? Is it that you need someone to look after the children while you are away from home? Or is it that you need a job with flexible hours to enable you to be home when the children are?

- If you are concerned about how you will look after a home and have a career, is the problem about how you will cope or how you can encourage others to help you?

- If you believe you are too old or too young, what exactly are you too old or too young for? Is the problem your age, the jobs you are targeting, your attitude to your age or other people's attitudes? They are all different problems, with different solutions.

Unless you have done some serious thinking about your perceived obstacles, you may still be in the dark about the specifics of your problem or even about the real problem itself. Solutions depend on you knowing exactly what you need.

SLEEPING ON IT

How many times have you gone to bed with a problem and woken up the next day with the answer? Or have there been times when an answer has come to you when you least expected it? Many people say they have woken up in the middle of the night with the answer to the thing that was puzzling them. It is often said that things will look different in the morning. It seems that the very process of shutting down the conscious mind allows the unconscious mind free rein to mull over the problem and come up with a solution or a different way of looking at things.

You may be puzzled by something that is holding you back from going in a certain career direction, or you may want to know if you should take a particular job or not. Sleeping on it might provide you with the answer.

Tapping into the resource

It is possible to tap into this resource by actually asking your unconscious before you go to sleep to solve a problem. It helps to state the problem out loud and not just think about it in your mind. Some people already do this by prayer. Whether or not you believe in God, a higher spirit or simply in the power of your unconscious, it is worth trying. What have you got to lose? Unfortunately, the answer does not always come immediately, so it is necessary to ask the question every night until it is solved. Some people have said it can take up to two weeks or so to get an answer.

How will you know you have the answer? It might just pop into your head, like a forgotten name often does, or you might be reading something and find that a certain paragraph is relevant to your problem. Alternatively, you may meet someone who gives you the answer. The trick is to stay alert to receiving the message in whatever form it comes. It is called trusting your unconscious, which after all wants the best for you.

FREEING UP THE UNCONSCIOUS

The conscious mind can only think of seven (plus or minus two) things at any one time. That is one reason why telephone numbers are quite difficult to remember if they are more than seven digits. We usually break them up into smaller sequences of digits so that we can remember them. When we are learning something, we learn first of all with our conscious mind.

Take driving, for instance. People learn a series of separate actions, such as turning on the engine, depressing the clutch, engaging first gear, looking in the mirror, signalling, disengaging the clutch, driving off – about seven actions in all. When we have learnt to drive, we do these actions automatically, seemingly without thinking. Some people then add more actions (not always legal), such as using a mobile phone, eating a sandwich, talking to a passenger, and so on. This is only possible, once the basic actions have been passed to the unconscious mind to be taken care of. If this is hard to believe, think about how often you have driven from A to B and not remembered any of the route you took.

The unconscious mind is very powerful. We need to take care of the million and one other things we are not aware of at a conscious level. For example, we take for granted just walking or eating. We do not think about each individual muscle action which enables us to walk or eat. So the unconscious mind is very powerful and very necessary. There are many ways we can tap into its power, some of which are mentioned below. What other ones can you think of or do you already use to free up your unconscious mind?

Doing something different

When you are struggling with something, such as writing a report, filling in an application form or drafting a business plan, it can help to stop what you are doing and do something completely different. If at work, change tasks, get up and take a walk round the office, talk to colleagues, make a cup of coffee. If at home, go for a walk, do some gardening, read a book or listen to some music. This allows your unconscious mind to deal with the task you have put on hold, while you distract your conscious mind from it.

By literally getting up and moving, you are giving yourself the opportunity to become 'unstuck'. Have you ever sat with pen in hand, or fingers poised over a keyboard, and no words would come? Often by simply moving your hand as if you were writing or typing, it gives a message to your unconscious mind to come up with the missing words. They may not at first be the right ones but at least you are making some progress!

Some people advocate breaking patterns to shake up your unconscious mind (eg brushing your teeth with your other hand, putting your other leg into trousers first, doing things in a different order).

Doing ordinary things differently may set your mind to thinking about problems in a different way. Change can be good.

Brainstorming

Brainstorming is an excellent way of freeing up the unconscious mind. Whatever the problem or task, take a piece of paper and write down any solutions that pop into your mind. If your inner voice starts saying 'yes, but that won't work' or words to that effect, ignore it and carry on making your list as long as possible, letting your imagination have free rein. It helps to believe that anything is possible at this stage.

You can brainstorm on your own or you can bring in other people. The rules are that no one should challenge an idea or ask for explanations until you have all run out of steam. Keep the flow of words going. Make it a game. Often the sillier the ideas, the better it is, as laughter stimulates the imagination and sparks off other, maybe more realistic, ideas. Have you ever thought 'well, actually, that's not so daft, particularly if you look at it this way...'? When your list is finished, then you can look at each item in turn and decide how realistic or possible it is.

Nowadays, there are many word or letter magnets on the market. These are very useful for stimulating the imagination or stirring up the unconscious mind. Some writers use them to play around with words or to inspire creative thoughts. See if it works for you.

Engaging the whole brain

It is possible to engage the whole brain in tapping the unconscious mind by using mind maps, learning maps or nuclear note making. These are popular ways of getting ideas to flow. They involve using both sides of your brain – the left (the logical, analytical side) and the right (the more imaginative and creative side). You usually begin with a central idea on a piece of paper and work outwards in all directions, creating a pattern of branches and sub-branches of thoughts and ideas. By using colour, drawings and symbols to capture your ideas, you are engaging your right brain. Your left brain can then begin to make logical associations between the different ideas. It is a way of working that represents and replicates how the brain works, with its millions of cells all connected to each other.

CHANGING THINGS ROUND

Changing attitude, changing language

In previous chapters, you have been encouraged to look at situations in different ways, to change your attitude towards them. For example, a problem could be seen as a challenge to be overcome, a solution to another problem or as the end of the world. It all depends on your point of view. The Chinese extend this to their language, by apparently having the word for crisis meaning both opportunity and threat.

If you could reframe some or even all of your limiting experiences into something more useful, how much would that change your life? No doubt your language would start to change, as your thoughts changed. You might become a more positive person as a result and attract more positive fortune towards you. Why not begin to think how you could do things from now on, instead of how you could not? Start the process by changing your language whenever you catch yourself saying 'no, I couldn't do....' or 'that wouldn't work' into 'I wonder how it would be if I could...' and 'how could I make it work?'

Changing perspectives

Remember when you were a child and everything seemed possible? Problems were just brushed aside as inconsequential. If you were a magician and could wave your magic wand, what would happen? Have fun fantasising that you are a child again or that you have a good fairy or a 'Mister Fixit' on your side – what imaginative ways forward can you come up with now?

By imagining how someone else would solve a problem, you are actually putting some distance between you and it. This always helps in gaining a different perspective. It is similar to sleeping on the problem, where the distance is time.

LISTING SOME CHOICES

Using some of the techniques listed above, it is now possible to go back to those obstacles mentioned in the previous chapter and see what kind of solutions might work.

- **No money:** how many ways can you think of to get some? Who do you know who might invest in you? How could you convince them? Use your charm, plans and enthusiasm. Do a proper business plan with all the calculations and reasonings and persuade a bank to lend you money. Could you move to a smaller house? Take in a lodger? Get a part-time job? Trade your skills for something else you want? Take an extra job, save more money if at all possible?

- **Children:** could you work from home? Could you start up your own nursery? Could you negotiate with your employer for flexible working hours? Could you job share with someone else who has children and each look after the other's when you are not working? (Recent research carried out in California found that working fewer hours does not hinder career progress.)

- **Partner and friends:** get them on board. Set aside quality time. For instance, even if you need or want to work or study in the evenings, it is still important to have frequent breaks. Accelerated learning teaches that having breaks allows the mind to assimilate the information and allows the unconscious to work on ideas. These breaks can be used to spend time with others. Agree to have at least one period of time daily completely free from work.

- **Looking after the home:** ask for help from all the family or pay for help if possible. Let your standards slip a little. Quentin Crisp once said that once dust reaches a certain height, you do not notice it any more. Shirley Conran, author of *Superwoman*, said that life was too short to stuff a mushroom. Have a takeaway meal every now and again instead of cooking.

- **Ageism:** think about how you could change someone's attitude to your age, making a virtue of it, perhaps by giving them a list of all the advantages in employing someone younger or older (whatever your situation) and conveying your enthusiasm, skills or experience. Even if you are 60, you still have five years of employment left – a long-term commitment in recruitment terms. Apply for jobs even when an age limit is stated. Aim to wow them with your personality. Look for jobs where ageism is not an issue.

- **Lack of training and skills:** find out how easy it is to get them. What do you have to do – specifically? Get all the information you can and give yourself the challenge of finding out as many different ways as possible of becoming trained and skilled.

- **Lack of opportunity:** how are other people finding jobs? Can you find someone to give you work experience (even without pay if necessary), or a temporary job that might then lead on to something more permanent? Is there voluntary work you could do to build up your experience and skills? Is there any retraining you could do?

The above shows just a very few of the ways you could think about obstacles and give yourself more choices. Remember these are just some answers and not necessarily the ones that will work for you. Once you have done some creative thinking of your own, it is possible you will hit upon the right solution for you.

CASE STUDIES

Robbie thinks creatively

Robbie wanted very much to be a radio DJ. However, he could not persuade anyone to give him an opportunity to show them what he could do. So he set his mind to thinking creatively. He entered a radio quiz on pop music. He won and while he was on air, he asked if he could swap his prize for a week's work experience. He not only got the week's experience, he also got the prize!

Rosie looks at all the choices

Rosie was in a dead-end job and wanted to get out. However, she needed a degree qualification to do what she wanted; she had a young baby to look after and no spare time or money. She discussed it all with her husband and friends and eventually they came up with a solution. She managed to get her company to sponsor her while she did her degree; she negotiated with her boss so that she could rearrange her work load to enable her to attend classes once a week. She had her husband's full support at home, so that they shared looking after the baby and the house, allowing her to complete her degree.

Suraj changes his attitude

Suraj was suddenly made redundant. He had no idea what to do. He spent days brooding on how unfair it was and how his life was now ruined. An uncle gently suggested that he begin to look on it as an opportunity rather than a disaster. He was now free to pursue whatever he wanted. He even had some money in the bank to put into a new venture, if that was what he wanted to do, or to enable him to take time out to think about his future. How many people have that kind of luxury? Once Suraj started to think in these terms, his whole attitude changed. He felt more positive about his future and began by asking friends and family for ideas on what he could do.

CHECKLIST

1. Have you identified your particular problems or obstacles?

2. How many ways can you think of to tap into your unconscious?

3. What habits or patterns do you have which you can break, just to do something different?

4. Have you tried looking at things from a totally different perspective, like a child's?

5. Soak up all the ideas you can.

6. How much can you change your language and your attitude to things?

7. Expect and embrace change.

10

Looking after Yourself and Your Career

When you are contemplating making some changes to your life, it helps to be in the best physical and mental condition. Often when people are concentrating on a particular part of their lives, such as a career, it is easy to neglect other areas and become out of balance. If you are out of balance, you may also be finding it difficult to be in control. This chapter gives you suggestions on how to take care of both mind and body and reminds you of why you picked up this book in the first place.

FOCUSING ON THE MIND

Feeling good

Do you always have to give yourself a reason for feeling good? Why not feel good for no good reason? Practise this right now. Just feel good about yourself, your life and your career (whether you have a career now or aim to have one in the future). No doubt if you did this, you smiled either externally or internally and your shoulders relaxed, releasing any tension in you. The mind and body are connected so if you feel good, your body will respond accordingly.

Tuning in to your highs and lows

Everyone has peak hours when they are more energetic. Notice when your high and low points occur. Leave more challenging tasks for when you are feeling energised and focus on routine tasks when you are feeling less sharp.

Paying attention

Be mindful – give all your attention to what you are doing. Practise the art of 'mindfulness' with simple activities that you would normally do without thinking: eating your breakfast, putting out the rubbish. By doing this you will find you notice more around you and within you and become more aware of the senses you sometimes take for granted.

Empowering solitude

If you are all fired up ready to take control of your career, it is vital to integrate some alone time into your day. There is no need to make a big deal out of this – simply closing your eyes on the train on the way to or from work, taking a walk at lunchtime or having a long bath can work. It can be empowering to realise you can enjoy being with your own thoughts. And you might come up with some bright ideas too!

FOCUSING ON THE BODY

Obviously a good diet, lots of sleep and exercise are important if your body is to respond in the way you need it to. It is also useful to do some or all of the following:

- Spend several hours each week doing something you love. It may be something you have previously thought is a waste of time or an indulgence. This gives you more balance in your life.

- Take time to engage in leisure activities every day: read a book, go for a walk, play a game or sport, listen to music.

- Learn to relax by breathing deeply two to three times and letting tensions release with the outbreath. Try relaxation tapes, yoga, meditation.

- Treat your body occasionally: have a meal out, have a massage, have a lie-in – whatever works for you.

MANAGING STRESS

It has been estimated that 30 per cent of people at work are suffering from stress at any one time. How do you react to a busy day? Do you:

- feel pleasure or distress?

- find you are alert or confused?

- find time is on your side or running out?

- find it easy or hard to make decisions?

- find it impossible to say no?

- feel overworked and out of control?

Your answers to the above will determine whether you are allowing stress to be your friend or foe. Two of the most common causes of stress are the demands we place on ourselves and the feeling of powerlessness to make changes. Some degree of stress is beneficial, making us more alert. It helps us to work to deadlines and perform well. Problems start when our brains overreact to stress and we feel we cannot cope with the smallest mishap. It is not the situation that is stressful but our reaction to it.

Preventing stress

The most effective cure for stress is **prevention**. Learn how to be kinder to yourself (see mind and body on pages 102 and 103) and you will soon feel you are once again in control of your life and your career. You could also:

- focus on a **single step** rather than on an entire task. This is much less stressful.

- aim to be **less than perfect**. Setting out to do everything to a level of perfection often means that jobs do not get done at all. Better to aim at doing a good job or the best you can.

- ask for **help** with prioritising, getting things into perspective, or with organising a more realistic work load.

- **write down how you are feeling**, especially if there is no one close by to talk to. This often helps put things into perspective.

- say **'no'** occasionally.

- aim for **balance** in your life – work *and* play are as important as each other.

Taking time out

Short breaks

To function most effectively, your brain needs regular breaks. Ten minutes is not going to alter things too drastically and it might just clear your head so you can start again refreshed. It often happens that if we do not take regular breaks, our unconscious mind decides we need them and we either lose concentration or become ill – anything that makes us realise we need to stop what we are doing and do something else.

Longer breaks

Some enlightened employers allow their staff to take sabbaticals, recognising that it is better to have fulfilled and happy staff than to lose good people. Some jobs lend themselves more readily to taking time out than others, for example, creative and people-related careers, where personal talents are more important than acquired skills. Would this work for you? Taking time out might allow you to take control.

COPING WITH CRITICISM

In previous chapters we have looked at obstacles standing in the way of you taking control of your own career and moving towards your goals. Sometimes it is other people's criticism of your ideas that stops you from doing what you want. The technique in Activity 13 teaches one way of coping with such criticism.

Activity 13 – Coping with criticism

This activity works best when you have practised it several times with remembered criticisms. You are then more able to do it automatically and quickly whenever you feel you are being criticised.

1. If someone criticises you or your idea, take a step back (in your mind) and imagine seeing yourself and the other person from a distance.

2. Now pretend there is some kind of barrier (maybe a perspex screen) between the 'you' watching and the other 'you' being criticised. This means you cannot experience any unpleasant feelings because you have literally distanced yourself and protected yourself with the barrier.

3. From this vantage point you can now decide whether the criticism is justified and if not, what its meaning could be.

4. You can then decide on a possible, evaluated, response to the criticism, without having to react in the heat of the moment.

5. Practise doing this in your mind, by remembering past times you have been criticised. Notice how different it feels when you distance yourself.

REMINDING YOURSELF WHY

Remember why you picked up this book? You were obviously thinking about making some changes in your life. Now you have got this far, are you going to find a whole new set of excuses for not moving at all from where you are? Or have you decided that this is going to be the year when you grasp the nettle and take some action to do what you want?

If you want to be in control, you have to put some effort in. The sooner you start, the sooner you will be going in the direction you want.

This book, like life, represents a wonderful opportunity or a waste of time, depending on what you do with it. You benefit only to the extent you use it and carry out the activities in it, learning about yourself and how you might achieve your goals. You have now put together the essential ingredients for success: **self-knowledge, vision, planning, persistence, a belief in yourself and your right to success.** You are therefore free to follow your dream – and take control of your own career.

Enjoy yourself. It is later than you think. Why wait any longer?

CASE STUDIES

Tom deals with stress

Tom was late for an important meeting; his car would not start so he had to get the train which was delayed en route. Walking from the station it started to rain and he had not got an umbrella. Then he remembered he had left important papers on his desk which he needed for the meeting. What did he do? Instead of telling himself that it was going to be one of those days and feeling totally overwhelmed and that the whole world was against him, he did something different for a change. He phoned his office and asked a colleague to fax over his papers; he phoned the person he was meeting and explained he was delayed; he popped into a nearby store and bought an umbrella. He told himself today was going to be challenging but productive.

Emily gets back on top

Emily was in a high-powered job, working in advertising, which she really enjoyed.

However, she felt she was close to 'burn out' and desperately needed some time out to recharge her batteries. She persuaded her boss it was better to give her two months off rather than have her resign and have to find a replacement. She went back to work full of renewed energy and bursting with lots of ideas. She felt back in control again.

CHECKLIST

1. Be kind to your mind: feel good for no good reason.

2. Be kind to your body: incorporate regular rest periods in your life.

3. Remember to use constructive rather than destructive self-talk.

4. Keep your mind on what you want to achieve rather than on what you do not want to happen.

5. Take one step at a time. Small, achievable goals will get you closer to your final goal.

6. People who regard change as an opportunity, not a threat, have the most success.

7. Take control and create the working life you want.

8. Read through all the activities in this book again. If they feel wrong, ignore them. If they feel right, act on them – and enjoy yourself.

9. Just do it.

Glossary

Access course. For people who want to go on to higher education but who do not have the necessary entry qualifications.

Affirmation. Positive statement in the present tense.

Anchoring. A stimulus that consistently produces the same feeling.

As if. Pretending something were true and acting and thinking as if it were.

Brainstorm. Stream of (un)consciousness.

Business Link. Government funded agencies providing information and guidance to new and existing small businesses.

Chunking down. Breaking down into smaller steps.

Creative visualisation. Using mental imagery to create positive changes.

DfEE. Department for Education and Employment.

Guided visualisation. Distracting conscious mind with a story or metaphor.

Key skills. Communication, numeracy, information technology, teamwork, problem-solving.

NLP. Neuro-Linguistic Programming.

Reframing. Changing the frame or meaning of an event.

TEC/LEC. Training and Enterprise Council (England and Wales) and Local Enterprise Companies (Scotland): government funded agencies responsible for coordinating government training and enterprise projects in regional areas.

Transferable skills. Skills not specific to any one job but which can be adapted to suit different working environments.

Treasure collage. Visual representation of dream and goals.

Further Reading

HELP WITH YOUR CV/CHOOSING A CAREER

Writing a CV that Works, Paul McGee (How To Books).
The Which? Guide to Choosing a Career, Barbara Buffton (Which? Books).

LABOUR MARKET INFORMATION

Labour Market Skills and Trends (Skills and Enterprise Network, DfEE). http:/www.open.gov.uk/dfee/skillnet/senhome. htm.

INSPIRATIONAL

Creative Visualization, Shakti Gawain (New World Library).
Dare! Wendy Grant (Element).
Feel the Fear and Do It Anyway, Susan Jeffers (Arrow).
Living Magically, Gill Edwards (Piatkus).
Man's Search for Meaning, Viktor Frankl (Washington Square Press).

NLP-RELATED STARTER BOOKS

Awaken the Giant Within, Anthony Robbins (Simon & Shuster).
Heart of the Mind, Connirae Andreas and Steve Andreas (Real People Press).
Introducing NLP, Joseph O'Connor and John Seymour (Thorsons).
NLP, The New Art and Science of Getting What You Want, Dr Harry Alder (Piatkus).
Unlimited Power, Anthony Robbins (Simon and Schuster).

Index